Straight to Great
THE SALES MANAGER'S FIELD GUIDE

by Jeffrie Story

"The best sales tool in the world is a great sales manager."

Bruce Mihok, Vice President of Digital Marketing
Global Marketing, Inc. at SAP

To Janae and Andrew,
Always the first to alert me and laugh
when I'm eating bricks

Acknowledgements

Straight to Great comes from three primary sources:
- My years of doing, learning, succeeding and making mistakes in corporate America, where I was a sales person, a sales manager, and a director of sales and marketing. I especially acknowledge all the salespeople who may have suffered through my growth curve!
- The ongoing research and expertise on call reluctance from George W. Dudley and Shannon L. Goodson, founders of Behavioral Sciences Research Press, Inc. (BSRP) and authors of the world-wide best seller *The Psychology of Sales Call Reluctance®[1]*. Now a licensee for BSRP, I have been able to view my personal career experience from a totally different perspective and add significantly to my clients' results, whether through better hiring decisions or training or coaching or consulting.
- My clients, who continue to help me grow, whether they realize it or not. Being able to immerse myself into their businesses, their challenges and goals, as well as work with every level of their sales organization, always helps me learn more. There is never a one-way street when we interact with others.

---

1   George W. Dudley and Shannon L. Goodson, *The Psychology of Sales Call Reluctance®* (Dallas: Behavioral Sciences Research Press, Inc., 2007)

Table of Contents

Part II: Managing and Coaching:
It's All Up to YOU

Part III: Critical Stuff to Spread Around

Part IV: Your Big MACK – Managing Action & Change Kit

PART I
Behaviors: Action in the Market

Tomorrow is often the busiest day of the week.

Spanish Proverb

CHAPTER 1
Surely We're Smarter than Pigs

Think about a time you sent a sales rep to training. Let's call the rep Judy. Judy skated out of class with accolades from the instructor, and you then spent a truckload of your time getting her up to speed with the real world of products, selling, systems, policies, procedures. You then released Judy from your nest, sent her off into Get-Some-Customers Land, and waited for results to roll in. You're still waiting.

While this scenario is shortened and exaggerated—you obviously didn't sit around waiting for results—it hits home for thousands of sales managers every year. Imagine how company profits and our economy would soar if we could just get people to do what we trained them to do!

It makes me think of the last time I saw a pig up close. Really. I was visiting a childhood friend back in Iowa, where I grew up. My former classmate was giving me a tour of his farm and boasting about his prize-winning pigs. Having been a "sophisticated" town kid with no agricultural expertise whatsoever, I didn't question his pride and sincerity.

But then, over his shoulder, I noticed one of his beloved swine chomping away on... bricks. I'm not kidding. Chunks of broken bricks! The pig snorted contentedly, head down, munching away on morsels of masonry as if they were nutritional manna from heaven.

These were prize-winners? It seemed like strange behavior to me, especially since pigs are supposedly one of the smartest animals on the planet.

Then it hit me. I'm an animal, too, and I'm a member of the smartest species there is (presumably). Yet how often did I exhibit stupid behavior that didn't serve my best interests?

Only later did I realize such behaviors are more common than strange. Every day in my sales world, I saw sales reps losing time and energy to unproductive behaviors, and even doing their own form of snorting. I was even more appalled when I found myself snorting in some way or another.

Usually our revenue-stealing behavior has turned into habits that are so engrained we don't notice them. We all have them. Whether we're sales managers or sales reps, we can be like that pig I saw, who just kept gobbling away, not realizing he was eating bricks.

Sales reps can't control the outcome of individual opportunities, so their overall success is gained solely from the quality and quantity of their behaviors. When salespeople "eat bricks," they lose sales.

Today's Behavior Drives Tomorrow's Results

As you are well aware, revenue is achieved only *after* taking action. The only way to improve revenue in the future is to change behaviors *today*. By the time the revenue reports arrive, it's too late to take action to improve them. Regardless of how great a sales manager you may be, you can't turn time backwards.

Our costly behaviors can quickly develop into habits that are automatic and go unnoticed. Even when we're aware of them, they can be difficult to change, because they're either as comfortable as an old pair of sweat pants or as rigid as steel. So we have three issues with habitual behaviors:

1. We don't recognize them
2. They're comfortable
3. They're difficult to change

This could be good or bad, of course, depending on what results flow out of the behaviors. Unfortunately, our costly behavior can develop at a faster speed than our productive behaviors, just like it's easier to become a couch potato than a marathon runner.

I once started working with a several teams of inside salespeople from one company. They were calling businesses statewide. They had an almost-daily habit of leaving the office en masse for a mid-morning breakfast across the street. As soon as they saw Joe putting on his coat, a slew of reps closed up shop for almost an hour. They followed Joe as if he were the Pied Piper. One rep said to me, "Whenever I see Joe, I smell hash browns!"

Before we had barely begun our work together, their office was closed and all the reps were laid off. Apparently by the time it was their turn for training they had already eaten too many hash browns. Better stated, their managers hadn't curbed the hash brown habit.

Most habits we fall into aren't as obvious as this. Many are subtle and difficult to identify, which is why you, as sales manager, are personally so critical to success.

Think about behaviors you notice within your sales force day after day. Identify some of the habits, the level of urgency, the productivity, the selling quality, etc.

What's the speed of your team? Is it slow, or fast and frantic, or fast and effective?

Do you ever notice reps who are finding one excuse after another to avoid making enough prospecting calls or taking other essential action? Maybe they aren't even looking for excuses any more—they're just saying to themselves, "This is me," as they bite into their own version of bricks. If that's the case, you have a Gatherer culture for sure. You're also probably swimming for life in a raging stream of frustration.

If your team is speeding daily and effectively along the prospecting street, you have a remarkable Hunter culture, and your life is grandly abundant. These are rare.

Where does *your* team fall on the spectrum?

Most fall somewhere in between the Gatherer and Hunter cultures. Your group is moving along and prospecting, but not necessarily speeding with ease or as effectively as you want. They might be doing well, but you know there is more potential to be conquered. You may even wonder what's holding them back. You know something needs change but it's hard to pinpoint it, much less measure it. Maybe you call it a "sense of urgency" or some other characteristic. But what does that mean in terms of actual day-to-day behaviors?

This is where many sales organizations find themselves, and they can be vulnerable. Sales reps catch bad habits and attitudes from each other, often listening to someone replay a bad selling experience. Or from a peer who says, "Don't listen to that training (or that boss). This is how we do things."

And "this," I guarantee you, is not a behavior you want.

Most sales organizations also aren't filled with salespeople who are making the money they are capable of making. If they were, executives wouldn't be asking age-old questions about their sales forces like:

- Why don't our salespeople just do what we've trained them to do?
- Why don't they make more contacts?
- Why don't they prospect more?
- Why do they hide behind servicing?
- Why do they complain so much?
- Why don't they recommend more?
- Why don't they cross-sell more?
- How can I get them to change?

Like it or not, the responsibility falls squarely on the front-line sales manager – you. And you may already be overwhelmed with administration, meetings, servicing issues, reports, etc. and have no idea how to go about changing other people's behaviors and habits anyway!

Plus, sales managers in general aren't psychics or psychologists, even though many seem to expect you to be. This means you're asking yourself the same questions as the executives are asking you, which boils down to: Why aren't they selling more?

Can a sales force really change? Yes, it can, but it takes great focus on those things that create revenue. And what are those things? Actions, behaviors, habits. In these chapters you'll gain information and insights to help you do better what you were hired to do: get more revenue-producing *behaviors* from your sales reps.

Henry Kissinger said, "The task of the leader is to get his people from where they are to where they have not been." That's exactly what your role is. It is also your challenge, because it means you're a behavioral change agent.

And changing behaviors is how you can go straight to great.

CHAPTER 2
The Critical Link

YOU are a very critical link. A company's strategies come from the top; marketing massages them, creates products and brings them to life. But who makes sure they really get into the marketplace?

It's not the sales reps. Salespeople are the carriers, but you are *the critical link* to make sure they get implemented well, and that they're successful. Without you, as a direct line to the actions of the reps, all great ideas and plans can languish on paper in the clouds. Without you, the best strategies in the world can fail.

I recently attended a professional meeting on tools for sales organizations. There were four speakers discussing CRM's, social media tools and applications, etc. But one speaker drove it all home for me. Bruce Mihok, Vice President of Digital Marketing for Global Marketing, Inc. at SAP began his talk with this sentence: "The best sales tool is the world is a great sales manager." And he's exactly right.

This is a weighty responsibility. Why would you want it? Why are you a sales manager? Why aren't you a sales rep?

You probably have several inter-twining reasons, if you're like most sales managers:

- For a sense of accomplishment with something new
- To make a difference in the lives of others
- To make more of a difference at your company

- Because you like being a leader
- As a stepping stone to reach higher goals
- Because something inside you says that's what you're meant to do
- And/or for the money, although many salespeople can earn more than their managers.

The purpose of this book is to help you improve the effectiveness of your sales reps, so that you, they and your company earn more. Even selecting one or two of the actions or ideas presented could make a big difference, especially if you suffer from the same issues as most sales managers in nearly every industry. These challenges include:

- Starting each work day feeling like you first need to cut through a deep fog, asking yourself:
  - What are my reps doing?
  - How productive are they?
  - Who needs the most help?
  - How can I best use my time?
- Having constant interruptions, and frequently leaving work feeling exhausted, yet having crossed very little off your To Do list
- An occasional or more-than-occasional feeling of overwhelm at all the non-sales work that comes across your desk or zaps in through cyberspace
- Lamenting the fact that your reps are not doing what they were trained to do, or that they aren't doing enough of it
- Wondering why your new rep John interviewed like a star but so far isn't producing squat.

And you might keep asking yourself:

Why won't they sell more?
What should I do about it?
How can I get them to change their behavior?

Talents + ACTION = Results
or
Be + DO = Have

Salespeople can be brilliant, skilled and talented, but if they don't take your products out into the market well enough or often enough, it doesn't much matter. And if you want to drive new behaviors with your reps, chances are that you'll need to change a few of your own, too.

As you read, ask yourself what you can change by only 1% or 2% that would make a huge difference for you. Or what one or two habits you could change that would transform your sales force culture to revolutionize the results your reps are producing. These are meaty questions you've undoubtedly pondered.

I'm not suggesting you'll receive rote answers in *Straight to Great*. There are no magic formulas, because the sales manager role is one of science, art, and connection. What this book provides is a tool for you to gain insights to further improve your managing and coaching skills through new perspectives, ideas and ways to create more of your own success.

Whether you end up transforming your sales team is not up to me—it's up to you.

One Way to Benefit from This Book

I don't know about you, but I've read many books that gave me about one line of memorable content. Part of the reason was how I read them. Here's what I suggest when you read *Straight to Great*.

First, peruse it for the big picture. Then start at the beginning and read one or two chapters per day. Each chapter is based on a different topic, so you can read them consecutively, or skip around. When something particularly applies to you or gives you ideas, make notes, track your ideas, highlight items, or fold down specific page corners. Then put it down, but allow your brain to soak in the content. How might it apply to you? What ideas does it give you? Reflect on what you've read while you're commuting or standing in line or brushing your teeth.

You may find that your brain creates superb ideas for you while you're doing something else. At the same time, start mulling around in your head your top ideas, and keep track of them.

Then develop your own action plan related to what you'll do and where you'll focus. Make a few focused changes at a time. You might change one habit, or you might take specific actions. Or you might alter where or with whom you're spending your time.

The following day, read one or two more chapters and follow the same soak-in-the-brain process. Take action as you read, or wait until you've finished reading to pull it all together.

In Part IV you'll find additional tools and thought processes to aid you, if you choose to use them. I call it your Big MACK—your Managing Action and Change Kit.

Once you're in the groove with one or two new actions or habits, move to the next one(s) you've chosen. It might take 30 or 60 days or even longer to complete your first actions, but you'll be moving upward and forward.

If you happen to fall off your plan, don't beat yourself up. Just review and/or modify your plan, dust yourself off and get back on track. Perfection is never a requirement, but action always is.

CHAPTER 3
The Habit Rabbit

There are some things that most of us trip over as we enter our workday, and we keep taking little spills all day long. These stumbles don't totally knock us over, so we ignore them, and soon they're just a comfortable part of each day. They become routines as predictable as morning coffee.

Although your role as sales manager is to drive behaviors that yield more revenue, we'd be remiss if we didn't examine our own habits and behaviors too. The primary reason is to free up more time for driving reps' behaviors.

What are these stumbles? They're our revenue-harming, stress-creating habits. Not only do they hurt us personally, they can set in motion similar habits in our employees.

With the global economy, competition and technological innovations bulldozing their way into our lives, most industries are digging deeper for ways to improve. There has never been a better moment in history for rooting out habitual behaviors that aren't serving us.

As you know, habits are *automatic* behaviors, and they're usually *unconscious.* We fall into hundreds of little behavior patterns every day. The question is whether they serve us or harm us.

Some destructive habits—those that keep us from achieving more revenue through effective managing and coaching—might include:

- Getting involved in helping colleagues with something that doesn't add to revenue generation
- Letting others interrupt us with discussions that could fill your Sunday newspaper's editorial section
- Working on items that are easy to cross off our lists but aren't our biggest priorities
- Chatting with other managers about non-essential issues
- Doing instead of teaching and delegating
- Checking e-mail multiple times each day or each hour, while telling ourselves we're being responsive and efficient
- Walking to the coffee pot or water cooler enough times to qualify as daily exercise. (My personal favorite.)

By day's end we feel like an exhausted habit rabbit, hopping from bush to bush in random directions. We haven't made the progress we know we can make; we haven't used all our energy and potential effectively.

It's a striking comparison with how exhilarated we feel on those too-rare days when we're "in the zone."

How much more powerful would we be if we were more conscious of our habits? If we changed just a wee bit, we might have time to sneak in more of the following:

- Asking reps some details about their prospecting challenges and successes
- Digging in to help someone with a proposal
- Sampling customer notes to determine how well reps are handling needs analysis with prospects
- Analyzing results to determine which people need more coaching
- Determining where you have holes in multiple product selling, then uncovering the causes and taking action
- Doing even five more minutes of coaching or call observation
- Calling a few customers to find out how you can bring them more value and benefits.

I find that these good habits listed above are the most frustrating ones for sales managers to develop because they so often can't find time to do them. Yet how can we expect sales reps to find time for more prospecting if we can't find time for more coaching?

What ideas are popping into your mind at this point? How costly are they? Which one would have the best payback if you changed it?

The challenge is not caused solely because we're drowning in habits that don't serve us. The front-line sales manager has, without doubt, one of the most difficult yet important jobs in the world. It's precisely why rooting out interruptive habits is such an important endeavor.

Challenge yourself to identify and avoid just one daily stumble into the snare of the habit rabbit, and head toward finding your best zone. There's one with your name on it.

CHAPTER 4
Renting Behavior

Do you ever feel like your company owns you? And do you also feel like you own "your" reps? We often feel that way, especially on bad days, or when we feel stuck with low achievers and don't know what to do.

There is an underlying concept I've discovered called *renting behavior*. It helps to keep it at the front of your mind every day, especially in sales management. No one owns anyone at work; we are merely renting behavior of others, and our company is renting *our* behavior too.

I latched on to this concept of renting behaviors years ago while in a diversity workshop at the corporation where I was working. The company was trying to work itself out of class action lawsuits and keep the government happy by making sure equality thrived (although I'd like to believe the purpose was more altruistic). At one point a participant complained, "But I can never get some of my employees to believe differently!"

The facilitator answered with words that rang deep within me. He said, "Employees can believe whatever they believe. We're not forcing them to change their beliefs. All we're doing is renting their behavior, and *that* is something we can require."

What a powerful concept! We don't have to beg, bargain, threaten and cajole to change *people*—we can simply rent behaviors that produce results.

But how often do we say something like, "Go get results! You need to meet quota!"

It's a paraphrase of what most sales managers say to salespeople at some point or another, if not daily. We view our jobs as managing people to meet and surpass financial objectives. And that's true. Yet it's our managing and coaching of behaviors that drive results even farther.

When you hired your salespeople, you didn't hire their results. You made an unspoken contract to rent their behavior. You rented what they *do* in the market.

When you reward your top salespeople, aren't you in actuality rewarding the behaviors they took to deliver those results?

When a salesperson gets what we used to call a "bluebird"— a company moving into town that brought in easier sales, for example—don't you mentally discount just a wee bit your praise of that salesperson? After all, he/she didn't have to work as hard for it. In other words, that sale didn't require all the behaviors that most sales require. The sales rep's peers are well aware of this, too, so that big sale doesn't necessarily inspire them to change their own behaviors.

If you rented a car and it wouldn't turn left, what would you do? You'd insist your car drive the way you wanted it to drive. After all, it's your money.

In a similar manner, you have every right to rent specific behavior from your salespeople.

Too often managers don't take full advantage of their rental agreement with salespeople. They tell their salespeople to "go get the results," and then they reward them when, or if, they succeed. When it comes to behaviors, they *suggest* instead of requiring. Or they require behaviors they can't measure or follow up on consistently.

In many cases we're dealing with reps' habitual behaviors that have been etched as deep as the Grand Canyon, and often those habits don't serve their revenue results.

The critical action, of course, is to expect behaviors that will lead to successful results. Yes, you might get some resistance from them at first, but employees do want to do a good job. Once the new behaviors start reaping benefits, and habits start changing, their attitudes will change even more.

You can require written proposals, that sales reps initiate a predetermined number of new business calls, that they open existing accounts for cross-selling, that they always tell customers about special promotions, or that they plan and prioritize their day. Whatever legal and ethical behaviors you want, you can rent.

Make a short list of behaviors you need from your sales organization, and ask yourself: Are these behaviors that you want to require as part of your rental agreement?

You also don't need to rent the exact same behaviors from everyone. If Mary is struggling for a different reason than Mario, you can decide what behavior to rent from each of them. Just change only one or two actions at a time, so they can focus their energy until cementing the new habit.

Then… and here comes the golden moment… you communicate it. Instead of saying, "Charles, you need to contact more prospects," you determine exactly what you want Charles to change. It might be as simple as making three appointments before he does anything else each day.

You can also communicate the concept of renting behavior. You might think this would be threatening or too controlling, but it isn't.

For example, you could say, "Nancy, I want you to succeed. But I don't own you, and I don't own your beliefs. I just rent your behavior. Here's what I do need to rent from you." Won't that sound reasonable to the salesperson? Maybe even liberating, because one wants to feel owned.

An essential element is to be very specific, so you can spot-check and reinforce. You'll want to follow up frequently, especially at first. If you don't follow up, your words of wisdom will evaporate into hot air.

At its core, your job is to drive behaviors, just as General George Patton's was. He must have understood behavioral management very well. I can picture some of his field captains complaining about their troops when he said, "If you can't get them to salute when they should salute and wear the clothes you tell them to wear, how are you going to get them to die for their country?"

Fortunately, the only war you're waging is a behavioral one, and the only enemy is inside each one of us.

Use your managing and coaching energy to rent behavior, and your salespeople will start listening and taking action. For any who refuse action and continue to struggle with results, it might be time to rent a different car. Or as one of my clients would say, "It's time for that rep to seek excellence elsewhere."

CHAPTER 5
The Vital Denominator of All Selling

After leaving my corporate sales director job for sure-to-be greener pastures, I began discussions with a prospect who ran an inside sales organization. They had around 500 salespeople, and my excitement was bubbling. My prospect spent considerable time on the phone with me (they were in another state), explaining their sales goals and challenges, and I knew in my heart that I could help make a big difference in their results. We then set a phone appointment for the proposal.

I proceeded to spend *hours* writing the perfect proposal. It was an *object d'art*. I sent it off prior to our phone meeting, feeling quite proud of myself. *This is easy and so fun!* I thought. At the appointed day and time, I placed the anticipated call to my prospect, expecting him to be excitedly poised by his phone.

But he wasn't. In fact, I was never able to reach him, either by email or phone. He blew me off. I was devastated and confused.

Needing moral support, I called my daughter Janae, who is also in sales, and complained, "I spent so much time on that proposal and they wouldn't even *take my call or talk to me! Can you believe that?*"

After several minutes of my lamenting and sniveling, she interrupted me. "STOP WHINING!" she yelled. She then uttered something that will always stay with me: "Your *job* is to write proposals, so get back at it!"

This story demonstrates many lessons about what not to do, including how we can get too involved in outcomes at the expense of monitoring behaviors. And that quality cannot make up for quantity—we need both. It's too easy to forget, and we can get emotionally involved at the expense of the big picture.

As I've thought about that moment since, and worked with many sales reps and sales managers over time, I've realized repeatedly that we need to keep visible the concept of combining quantity of behaviors with quality of behaviors. It's a crucial balancing act.

To keep that message churning in the heads of salespeople, let's dig into the key role of a salesperson.

If we polled all the grade school children in any modern country and asked them what they wanted to be when they grow up, I doubt if many would say, "I want to be a salesperson!" Maybe none of them would. Most of us fall into sales while looking for a job, or we accept a sales position as a stepping-stone to something else. Often we don't have an inkling of what a salesperson really does until we start the job.

Depending on what kind of sales position we're hired to perform, we soon find there are many functions within that job. You've probably had newly hired people ask indignantly, "You mean I have to do THAT?"

We might be responsible for customer service, placing orders and doing other administrative work, asking questions, implementing, tracking, negotiating delivery dates, escalating problems, learning about products and benefits and value, presenting products, writing proposals, etc. Some of these functions and tasks are enjoyable or tolerable; others are nuisances and even dreadful.

But there is one crucial function that all sales jobs have in common. That function is hunting for prospects we can turn into customers. We're all supposed to be "writing more proposals" in some way. Whether we're in call centers or inside sales, direct sales, national account sales, or customer service, we're looking for prospects who will buy from us, or buy more than they already buy, or stay with us longer.

The prospecting function could also be called Customized Advertising. This twist of words can give the salesperson, and the sales manager, a more focused, strategic and reality-based approach.

When a company designs its advertising budget, they first ask themselves several questions, such as:

- How can advertising support our company goals?
- What are the key reasons people would buy from us? What needs or wants are we filling?
- Why should prospects select us over our competitors? Do we surpass our competitors in price, or service, or innovation, or value?
- How can we turn our strengths into a compelling and unique selling statement that clearly gets our message across?
- How can we keep our message in front of the maximum number of most-likely buyers (the target market), without paying too much?
- And of course, what are the best types of advertising we can mix together (the media mix) for the best results?

Sales managers and executives ask themselves the same basic questions in relation to their sales organization. You begin with a "headcount budget," or something similar, and you determine how to get the most revenue, market share and customer loyalty from it.

At a sales manager level, you do the same thing, and you hopefully update it as markets and market potential change. You might re-align territories; you might add inside sales support as a cost-effective way to help outside salespeople; you might set up an outbound calling group for selected prospects or products.

Let's take this analogy to the level of salespeople. Think of them as an advertising vehicle, except that they are customizing their advertising for each prospect. What do we want advertising to do? We want it to reach enough of the right people at the right time with the right message, and then motivate them to take action by buying from us.

How do salespeople gain knowledge for customizing this advertising? By asking questions. This is the step that too many sales reps short-change by jumping into product features or pricing, believing prospects will take their own mental leap into value and benefits. In fact, I don't believe I've ever talked with a sales manager or executive who didn't want their reps to ask more questions, to dig deeper.

This statement obviously depends on the market, the sales cycle, the product, etc. If you're selling water in a park on a hot day, the need is obvious. Forget the questions and go for the close.

Let's put this customized advertising concept into a model that you can use with your sales reps.

Advertising has three general functions: (1) to inform, (2) to persuade, and (3) to remind. We're going to add two more functions, which advertisers perform also, but which sales reps perform at a more granular, individualized level. The first one is: to investigate, whether it's in the form of preparation, research, asking questions, or all of these. The second is initiating contact or conversation—taking action! Our model for how the sales rep "advertises" now has five functions:

1. Initiating—prospecting, making appointments, taking initiative in performing all the other functions, from investigating through reminding
2. Investigating—fact-finding, doing needs analysis, learning about the customer!
3. Informing—presenting how your products fill the prospect's specific needs, and what the prospect's net value gain would be
4. Persuading—selling, answering objections, closing
5. Reminding—maintaining awareness of your branding, following up

Number One Most Important Behavior: Initiating

We've talked about quantity vs. quality, and that you want both. But which is more important, more critical? In general, the answer is quantity. Even if a rep has only one large account, initiating enough contact with them is paramount to success. To quote George Dudley at BSRP[2] :

> *"The hesitation to initiate contact*
> *with prospective buyers*
> *on a consistent daily basis*
> *is responsible for the failure of more*
> *competent, motivated, capable salespeople*
> *than any other factor.*
> ***Nothing else even comes close."***

This hesitation, or lack of contact initiation, is called Sales Call Reluctance® (discovered through research by BSRP), and we can measure a whopping twelve different types of behaviors that inhibit contact initiation.

You might say, "Well, duh, we all know it's a numbers game." But usually it's the Number One Issue that managers have with their sales reps' behavior, and it can affect every single type of sales organization.

You may have read about experiments in sales organizations to test the results of making x number of sales calls and asking, "You don't want to buy any _____ , do you?" In these studies, the results consistently proved that even with a shabby sales process, the quantity of contacts made the effort cost-effective. Imagine what the results would have been by combining quantity with quality!

So be sure your sales reps are focused on, and accountable for, both quantity and quality, but the King of Success—the *Dictator* of Success—is quantity. Just make sure you're sending them in the direction of your target market. Average apartment dwellers in New York City don't buy very many swimming pools.

Initiating is more than cold-calling or making appointments. Low levels of contact initiation, which are based on fears that aren't even conscious, go much deeper and can weaken the other four functions required of salespeople. We "initiate" when we ask about the customer's business or personal needs, when we recommend,

---

when we close, when we follow up, when we cross-sell, when we ask for referrals, and on and on. It can especially hurt the Number Two Behavior.

Number Two Most Important Behavior: Investigating

The Number Two Most Important Behavior issue that sales management usually states, in my experience, is getting reps to find out more about the customer. Asking more questions. You already know your company's benefits from better investigating. They range from saving time through effective qualifying, to having robust, targeted recommendations, to identifying more value for the customer, to gaining trust, to a higher likelihood of improved selling—even if the reps are clumsy with informing and persuading.

What salespeople usually don't realize is how much customers want them to know about their business or personal needs. Reps can be so preoccupied with their own performance on a sales call that they neglect the concerns of the prospect, especially if they know you're in the background, mentally counting the number of questions they're asking.

If Investigating is an issue for your sales reps, at your next team meeting you might ask your sales reps to brainstorm all the different reasons that *their customers and prospects* would want them, the sales reps, to ask questions. Have them state the reasons using words a prospect might use. In case you receive blank stares, or silence on your conference call, here are some items you can use to get the conversation flowing, in a business-to-business sales group:

- "I don't have time to do research on all the products out there. When a sales rep helps me sort through the maze based on my personal situation, I save time and get what I need."
- "It shows they're not just pitching products to me whether I need them or not."

- "It shows they care about getting me what I need or want, which increases my trust level in them. And that means I usually buy more from them."
- "If sales reps find out about my goals and needs, and then make sure their recommendation supports those goals and needs, I definitely pay more attention to them."
- "For me it's a criterion they must meet. If a sales rep doesn't want to find out about my specific needs, I don't want to learn about their products."
- "It's easier to remember the reps who care enough to ask about my business goals and challenges."

This simple exercise could generate a very rich discussion among your reps and could create a valuable awakening that will help drive new behaviors. Too often we get stuck in our own habits and behaviors and forget to evaluate the interaction from the prospect's perspective.

Number Three Most Important Behavior: The Final Word

No single style, or personality, or technique, or sales process has ever proven itself to be the guru of results. But by the end of the day or end of the month, the sales person still needs to bring home the bacon. This involves the Persuasion function, which many salespeople leave out, either because of a skill deficiency or a fear. In *The Hard Truth about Soft-Selling*, George Dudley and Dr. John F. Tanner, Jr. write:

> "Burn *this* into your brain: Selling *is* selling. A salesperson's job is not merely to fulfill customers' needs. It is to *sell* them the product or service that can help fulfill their needs. Need-fulfillment, wish-fulfillment, will-fulfillment, and other intangible warm fuzzies are the currency of advertising, not selling."[3]

---

3   George W. Dudley with Dr. John F. Tanner, Jr., *The Hard Truth About Soft-Selling*, Behavioral Sciences Research Press, 2005.

Persuading is a behavior you're renting, and it falls squarely on you to make sure that you're getting sufficient quantity and quality of it. Even with awe-inspiring initiating and questioning, the same mission remains: close the sale.

CHAPTER 6
Your Own Vital Denominator

We used an advertising analogy to describe the key function of a sales position, and a similar analogy holds true for managers, especially with the behavior of initiating contact. Your own message and priorities need to stay in front of your salespeople. So ask yourself: Where/how can I stay visible with salespeople in a way that drives more revenue?

After getting my first promotion to sales manager during my corporate career, my district manager was coaching me on driving different behaviors from my sales team. After he suggested how I direct the reps, I replied, "But I've already told them that." He responded with wisdom I've never forgotten, saying, "If it's worth saying once, it's worth saying more than once."

If you ever say to yourself, "I've TOLD them that!" but they're not behaving the way you want, then the message isn't getting through in the way that you want.

Or they don't like your message or don't feel like doing what you want. In those cases, there's not enough risk/reward for their inaction/action.

Or you're not following through with renting the behaviors you want, which delivers your message as well as a letter without a stamp.

And whose problem is it? Who has the responsibility for their behavior? You do. Whether you need to change behaviors or change people, you own the accountability.

One reason your ongoing visibility is so critical is that if your organization isn't consistently hearing a message from you, they start making up one.

I once gave a speech to a group of salespeople who seldom had outside speakers. It was a small company with 70 salespeople. The rumor the next day was that I was there because I was thinking about buying their company!

Sales reps can make up hidden agendas they think you have, or new directions they think you're going. More wasted sales time. What's even worse is that they can single-handedly waste everyone's time and inflame your entire sales culture.

If they're hearing your consistent message, there's less fodder for rumors and wasted time, and more direction toward sales.

The visible messages you need to keep repeating relate especially to:

- Your goals
- Your priorities
- And most importantly, what behaviors you want them to change, improve, decrease, or increase

You may think you're already communicating your key messages consistently, but it's worth reflection. Do they ask the same questions repeatedly? Do you answer those questions with care each time, or do you just quote baseball Hall of Famer Yogi Berra and say, "I wish I had an answer to that, because I'm tired of answering that question."

Do your reps fully understand your direction, and are they following it? What is the retention level of *your* advertising? If you gave your reps a pop quiz on your key strategies, would they pass?

And Don't Forget Your Boss

Some managers operate under the assumption that if they keep pulling the sales force wagon with all their might, they'll get the recognition they deserve. Not true.

If you didn't keep your boss informed about what you're doing in the market, how you're managing, coaching and improving, what will he/she think when your sales start soaring? "Jennifer's market sure is improving. Something good is going on with the economy in her region." Will Jennifer get credit? No.

Likewise, when you're performing magnificently but the economy in your region really *is* taking a plunge, what will your boss say then? "What is Jennifer doing out there? Sitting around waiting for orders?" Will Jennifer get blamed? Yes. Could it affect the level of support she receives for her team? Unfortunately, yes.

Here we are again, returning to contact initiation. We could also name it self-promotion, which BSRP defines as "making our talents and skills visible to those people who can help us reach our goals."[4]

The Importance of Role Clarification

Equally or even more important than understanding your strategies and goals, sales reps need to know what is expected of them. Behavioral psychologists call this "role clarification." Your visibility and your actions are the only route to role clarification.

You may be thinking, "Of course my reps know what we expect!" But you may be surprised.

In a survey I conducted for a client, I found that reps overwhelmingly understood and agreed with the organization's sales strategy. However, most were frustrated because they had little idea of how to implement it. They didn't understand their role within that strategy. Among those who felt they knew their role, there were widely differing interpretations, resulting in conflicting behaviors, animosity and lost sales. The great news is that this company was willing to ask the tough questions, which provided power to resolve issues. And the sales reps were thrilled that executives wanted their opinions.

---

4   George W. Dudley and Shannon L. Goodson, *The Psychology of Sales Call Reluctance*® (Dallas: Behavioral Sciences Research Press, Inc., 2007)

Mixed Messages

Also damaging to job understanding are the mixed messages reps sometimes receive. This would be a real no-no in advertising, and it is to you, too. But sometimes managers, and companies, don't realize they're sending mixed signals.

The most common complaint I hear from reps is, "Why won't they make up their minds? One minute they send us to training on consultative selling[5], and the next minute they tell us to hustle a particular product. Which do they want, for crying out loud?"

When asked this directly by reps, many managers then answer with the following: "Of course I want you to sell consultatively. But right now we need to meet this quota for our new product and we're behind." Or they tell them to do both types of selling at the same time, which is the goal, of course, but often sales reps feel they're being sent in two different directions.

This short-term dilemma happens so frequently that many reps have never learned to sell effectively from a bigger picture, thus missing revenue potential. You may think they're doing both at the same time, but chances are they're not. It not only affects revenue, but also market share, future growth, and customer loyalty.

Another potential area for confusion is product goals versus revenue goals. You probably need to have compensation incentives for strategic products, as well as overall revenue quotas and perhaps even market share.

But do reps know precisely how to meet both quotas seamlessly? Or are they saying, "I have product goals and revenue goals, but sometimes I have to choose one over the other. So I sell what gives me the best commission."

This is human nature, and it's why we have incentive plans. Incentive plans give the final jolt to job clarity. The good news about incentive plans is that they work. The bad news? They work.

---

5 The reference to consultative selling includes need-based selling, solution selling, etc., as distinguished from pure product selling. From my research, neither type is more superior, and frankly, I'm not sure there's a difference. What matters most is that the sales process is matched appropriately with the product and the market.

If your incentive plan has a small glitch, you can be driving behaviors in a way that is drastically different from expectations you advocate. It causes more confusion and is can hurt both your reps and your company.

I've also heard reps say, "I'm not competing against other companies—I'm competing against myself. My quota is based on revenue from the same month last year, regardless of what has happened in the market. If I had a great month last April, I can kiss off this April. In fact, I'll try to delay sales until May."

What can you do to clear up this role confusion? Ask your reps what doesn't make sense to them, if they aren't already complaining in every sales meeting. If they say something is amiss, believe them. Then take action, whether it's to explain, clarify or resolve.

You personally may not have the authority to modify a compensation plan, but you can certainly identify issues and make suggestions. You can also look for ways to require—to rent—behaviors that soften or reduce the negative impact of the compensation hiccup.

In the same way that reps are advocates of customers and your company, you are the point person between reps and your company. If helpful changes can't be made, explain why. What's important is that you're clearing the path for them to know exactly what you want them to do.

In every step you take, remember that you do hold a powerful key to everyone's success. Be sure to use it by keeping priorities visible and clear.

CHAPTER 7
Multi-tasking vs. Overlapping: The Difference is in the Goal

Did you know that multi-tasking comes from science fiction? And that every day your multi-tasking takes a future into the present?

Think of multi-tasking as a wondrous time machine, except this machine moves tasks—not people—from a future chunk of time into the present so that we can perform multiple tasks at the same time. Now put a caveat on the definition: all the transported tasks contribute to one single goal, such as effectively handling a customer call.

When I was a sales leader in call centers, we tested job applicants on how well they could multi-task. It was critical to success and profitability. If the applicants couldn't talk to customers, manipulate a ridiculously complex computer system, take notes, up-sell, figure prices, and input orders simultaneously, we wouldn't hire them.

It made sense, except for that ridiculous system. Multi-tasking saves time for the customer on the line and provides better service. Without it, you could never have enough headcount for call requirements—a company's call center would fill all their buildings and eat all the profits.

But multi-tasking has practically become a mantra in business. We hear the word bantered around like a badge of honor, and we often think we're being more productive because of it. Our definition of multi-tasking has erupted over its useful boundaries and escaped into unproductive, slippery slime—whether for a sales rep or a manager. Why? Because we have confused it with what I call overlapping.

Think of the last time you were in a meeting while participants had their heads down, presumably participating while they answered emails and texts from their phones. You'd swear they were praying to some digital god. That's not multi-tasking; that's overlapping!

Overlapping is the same type of time machine as multi-tasking, but the tasks serve *multiple* goals. See Figure 1 for a visual of what Overlapping feels like. Prepare to get dizzy.

Multi-tasking is good. Overlapping is not so good. It's one of the mug shots of something called Goal Diffusion, discovered by BSRP's research.[6] With Goal Diffusion, we bounce our focus from one goal to another, losing effectiveness and/or productivity in each task.

There are times, however, when overlapping can serve us, such as reading a book while waiting for a flight. We're utilizing the same time to accomplish two goals, but neither is compromised—unless we get so absorbed in the book that we miss our flight.

As you've probably concluded, overlapping can attack anyone. Watch for it, in yourself and your sales reps, and address it when you observe it.

For me personally, avoiding a fall into overlapping is my biggest challenge, and it's an ongoing one. The only way I avoid its assault is through constant vigilance. (One beneficial tool is to prioritize tasks, which is discussed later and also detailed in Part IV.)

The challenge is to balance two things at all times: (1) the goal, and (2) effective use of time. There are many ways to save time by multi-tasking, but a careless use of overlapping could sneak in to sabotage our success. So take control!

---

6   Behavioral Sciences Research Press, Inc., Dallas, TX

It's time for a quiz. In the following scenarios, determine whether you believe the time-transported tasks are: (A) good, (B) bad, or (C) dependent on the situation.

- You're with a customer who has a huge service problem. Simultaneously you are listening, taking notes, thinking of solutions, demonstrating understanding, empathizing and apologizing.
- While your boss is on the phone with you, you take advantage of the time to sort your files.
- You have an open-door policy and encourage employees to interrupt at any point, demonstrating you are always willing to help.
- You set your computer to check for email every five minutes, buzzing you each time an email arrives. You immediately stop to read and answer every single one.
- Your reps are frantically working on a highly important deadline. Simultaneously you raise their quotas and introduce a new compensation plan.
- You're in yet another meeting with your peers and you take advantage of the time by making your grocery list or beginning what's sure to be a best-selling novel.

If you have difficulty with any answers in the quiz, just email me. I answer all email within 35 seconds.

Figure 1

A Symbolic Picture of Overlapping

Count the Black Dots

CHAPTER 8
Sales Culture = Behavior
You are the Key

Do you ever wish you had a magic wand that you could sweep over your sales team? Just think of what you could do with that wand: create more energy, lower their complaints, make them more aggressive in the market, raise productivity and sales behaviors and sales?

Well, you have that magic wand. In fact, you *are* the magic wand. You can change the culture of your team. And what, pray tell, is a culture? It's the sense of "who we are and what we do and how we think." And what makes up a culture? Behaviors. Even thinking and talking are behaviors. And you are renting behaviors, right? Does that mean you are accountable for the culture of your sales team? To a great extent, yes.

Your company's culture doesn't have to change in order for your sales team's culture to change. You have a lot of untapped power you may not realize. We could call it your brand. We all have a brand—it's how others perceive us to be. Honest? Fun? Hard-working? Driven?

Your sales team has a brand, too, and you're the creator and energizer of it. What do other's say about your team as a whole? More importantly, what do you *want* others to say? Here are some example statements of the power and influence you have, and what you might want others to say:

- Brian's team is always the first to meet quota.
- If you work for Mary, you'll get plenty of help.
- You seldom find Joan's team wasting time.
- Why does Peter's team always seem to be so positive?
- Al's team does nearly all their servicing toward the end of the day. They get it all done, too!
- Grady's team always has the highest revenue per order. He's a stickler for cross-selling.

Although we can drive behaviors, we can't change is how someone thinks, or what someone believes. But once we change behaviors, our beliefs usually fall in line behind the behavior. Here's a simple example: When you first got on a two-wheeled bicycle, you probably thought, "I'll never be able to ride without these training wheels!" That's a belief, a thought. But one day, usually with the help of a caring parent, the training wheels were taken off, and soon you were saying, "I can ride a bike! I'm a success!" Your belief changed based on your actions and behavior. Change occurred not only in your skill level, but also in your concept of who you are.

Experts in corporate cultures say that it takes a long time to change an organization's culture. Habits and attitudes and processes are pervasive, and everyone plays a role in holding on to the status quo.

You personally, however, can shake up the status quo. *You,* as a behavioral change agent, set the tone and expectations that drive the culture of your own sales team.

But be sure you're sending your sales team's culture in the direction you want. One single management action can unleash a tsunami on the results or attitude of your entire organization.

Picture yourself changing a compensation plan that reps perceive as being significantly more difficult than the previous plan. If it's not designed well and communicated to the sales reps well, it can attack your sales culture. Time formerly spent prospecting transfers into complaining and looking for loopholes.

Ineffective policies, cumbersome processes, poor systems, etc. could also be affecting your sales culture. It pays to *really* listen to your reps, let them know you're listening, and evaluate what they're saying. Ask them for suggestions, especially for anything you can personally fix or improve. Even something as simple as changing the day of your sales meetings could produce a shift in attitudes.

If your sales team as a whole is disgruntled, you may be in for some eminent, substantial turnover in the troops. Or quiet sabotage you won't know about until it's too late.

Your mission as leader is to create an environment that adds energy, so that the job isn't something that deflates employees. If they enjoy their jobs, if they trust you, if they feel you have integrity and vision, if they feel treated fairly, if your actions match your words—then chances are you're creating a positive culture.

But I suggest you avoid saying, "Oh, I don't have a problem here." We can easily delude ourselves. Keep asking; keep verifying.

Job habits, both individually and as a team, can also contribute negatively. An outside team selling advertising was so rushed on their Tuesday 12-hour deadline day that most of them didn't eat at all during the entire day. Or they ate junk. It wiped them out and affected their productivity the rest of the week. They usually had a great deadline day but lost plenty of business-building the other days.

Their conclusion was that deadline day was their "productive day," and they physically coasted, or practically collapsed, the rest of the week. This was their culture.

After realizing their destructive habit and what it was costing them, they decided that planning ahead to put food in their cars wasn't such a nuisance after all. The sales manager even helped organize the food planning. It ended up paying off substantially the entire rest of the week. A part of their team's culture changed with something as easy as putting food in their cars.

Managers can positively influence both the culture and efficiency of their teams. Below are some examples of different types of ways.

- Have group prospecting time first thing in the morning, when most people have their highest energy peak for the day.
- Encourage healthy habits. Don't fill your office with doughnuts. Sugar highs are followed by energy lows. How about big, crisp apples, granola bars or yogurt for a change? Healthy food is even in vogue, and many people do eat it!
- Fix cumbersome processes or illogical policies that are sapping energy. If you can't fix them, at least acknowledge the issue and explain to the sales reps why the processes and policies are in place — it will still help.
- Build laughter into the day. It lowers stress.
- Stay abreast of what your salespeople are thinking about their jobs. Keep asking.
- Hire energetic salespeople with successful behaviors and habits, who can serve as additional role models within your team
- Manage your own mood, tone and maturity, regardless of the issue.

Most sales organizations have decent sales cultures, overall. The chances are good that you do, too. But that doesn't mean you can't keep making improvements that lead to more sales and less stress (which also leads to more sales).

You, not your company, are the key to fastest change.

CHAPTER 9
Hiring Hunters

Hiring salespeople is one of the single most impactful functions you have as a sales manager. Think about it: Your livelihood literally depends on the behaviors and actions of your sales reps, and how well they charge out and hunt. If you hire people who will do more naturally what your sales job requires, it makes all other your other managerial functions easier and more effective.

Employers often want to hire salespeople with industry background. Sometimes it's critical. The question is: will they do anything with that background? Will they use it to take off running once you hire them?

So you diligently get references, which may or may not be accurate. You certainly don't want to hire your competitor's mediocre performer who is looking for a greener cubicle or a better compensation plan.

I've observed many newly hired salespeople who don't have industry experience, much to the chagrin of the hiring managers. But some of these folks immediately start breaking down barriers where veteran reps had waived a white flag of defeat. They don't know what can't be done, so they go do it.

Yes, industry knowledge can be desirable or even crucial, but not if it's in the wrong person. Dr. W. Edwards Deming, the father of the revolutionary quality process said, "Does experience help? NO! Not if we are doing the wrong things." And not if we're avoiding doing the right things, or not doing enough of the right things.

If you're in a changing industry, you might gain positive culture shocks by hiring outsiders, but only if you're hiring well.

In your hiring function, you definitely want to accurately answer two questions:

1. *Can* they do it? (Aptitude, skills, experience, fit in company culture)
2. *Will* they do it? (Behavior in the market, drive, willingness to be coached)

Should you use formal assessments and testing in hiring? Absolutely. They are additional tools and provide more pieces to the puzzle. An interview, a resumé, recommendations and even previous sales results don't tell the entire story. Someone who appears assertive and determined may turn out to be bull-headed and disruptive, which I learned years ago through a hiring mistake.

I am a licensee for an assessment that answers question number two above: *Will* they do it? This assessment, the SPQ*GOLD®, which measures Sales Call Reluctance®, was developed by Behavioral Sciences Research Press, Inc. (BSRP). It predicts on a scale from zero to 100 how much a sales rep will produce, how soon they'll start producing, and how easy or difficult they'll be to manage. (For information on this assessment, you can contact me and I'll obviously be happy to talk with you.)

Regardless of what assessments you use, make sure they're grounded in enough research. All assessment providers will surely attest to high accuracy, so dig deeply. If they say it's "90% accurate," beware. Where does that 90% come from?

You can't afford assessments? Perhaps you can't afford *not* to assess. Too often we need the job vacancy filled immediately and we think we can't "afford" the luxury of holding off for the right person. But is this really a luxury?

What many managers and even companies don't fully realize or think about is the *real* cost of a hiring mistake. Some researchers estimate the cost of a faulty hiring decision can total five times the annual salary of the job position.

There are revenue costs and expense costs, as well as time costs that affect both revenue and expense. Most of the costliness has a hidden and undocumented component. Consider how the following elements decrease revenue if you've hired poorly:

- Recruiting time
- Formal training time
- Managerial time and coaching time
- Time diverted away from current employees
- Time to give the person a fair chance to succeed
- Energy diverted by company documentation and/or process requirements
- Revenue lost in the territory your mismatched employee is assigned
- Re-recruiting time

You can get attacked by a headache just reading through that list. But what about those mediocre performers who repeatedly slide by with minimum performance? Have you ever calculated what they're costing you?

Early Performance: The Great Predictor

Newsflash: The single greatest predictor of ongoing sales success is: Early sales performance.

Let's say you hire Lucy and train her. Three months later you deem her to be out of the shoot and into the race. Lucy performs in the middle of the pack. At the six-month mark, she's still a mid-performer. You start chewing your fingernails and wondering why you can't get her to do better. So you send her to get yet more training, and you spend more time with her, adding to your investment cost.

But here's the kicker: In 18 months, or 24 months, Lucy will still be performing in the middle of the pack. There is a near-perfect statistical correlation for her lack-luster standing, according to two separate research studies by BSRP[7].

---

7   Behavioral Sciences Research Press, Inc., Dallas, TX

When you predict early performance, you'll also be predicting later performance.

This has tremendous implications for hiring tools and practices. You could be hiring people who are mid-performers, lowering the bar for your company's potential. If everyone is at the same level of mediocrity, you obviously can't fire everyone and start over. And the saddest part is that you may not know about the missing potential, blaming it on the market.

How your sales organization performs, or how your top producers perform, is usually viewed as one indication of market potential. But is it? You could have a tremendous amount of market potential that you're limiting because of:

- Whom you hire
- Your compensation plan
- Management practices
- Management skill, focus or knowledge
- Territory assignment
- Internal systems and processes
- Lack of sales support

Notice that hiring the best-matched salesperson is at the top of the list. You've undoubtedly heard the mantra to "hire slow, fire fast," and of course it's true. By making sure you're hiring people who will sell, you've at least crossed off one of those factors that limits your market potential.

Whether you use the SPQ*GOLD® assessment or another assessment, or no assessment (gasp), make sure you ask a flood of questions about past behaviors in past situations. Look for behaviors based on your company's needs. Watch behaviors during the interview process. After all, you're not really hiring Lucy—you're hiring her behaviors.

CHAPTER 10
About Money

Some salespeople have dollar signs dripping off their foreheads. These dollar signs are good signs, as long as they're attached to effective and ethical behavior.

Other salespeople proudly state they're not driven by money. They just want to show up each day, "do their job," and go home with a sense of pride in their work. This is more prevalent with inside sales reps, and it's rampant in inbound call centers.

Others just want a sense of accomplishment; they want to use their innate potential and creativity; they want challenges and growth. And they're content to be just comfortable.

Here's the kicker: As sales managers, we're not doing a good job if we're not helping our companies succeed to the highest extent possible. If compensation plans are partly or wholly commission-based, which nearly all are, we need to make sure sales reps are focused on earning the most money possible, not just meeting minimum standards.

As your company's critical link to revenue, you're wise to emphasize the value of striving for money and that it's not the "root of all evil." We may think everyone realizes this, but we all have messages about money in our heads that stem from childhood. You'll find self-help books at the library designed to annihilate this money-sucking, invisible vampire.

How can we communicate a more humane or unselfish benefit of money, so that our reps' internal drive creates more lucrative behaviors? Below are some thoughts about the value of money. You can use these concepts and add your own when you find the need.

✳ ✳ ✳

When money is in your bank account or on your investment statement, regardless of the amount, it's just ink on paper or an online number.

Now hold some real money in your hand. What function does it serve? You can't eat it to conquer hunger; it won't keep you warm; it won't keep you dry in the rain. It's just dirty paper or metal.

But money is above all a means for emotional well-being. We feel better when we know we have it, because we know we can trade it for something we want or need. It sends happy messages to our brains, for many reasons:
- It keeps us from worrying about emergencies or price increases we can't afford
- It gives us a feeling of being safe
- It gives us more freedom and flexibility.
- We can give it away to people or causes we care about, which feels good
- When we plan that family vacation to Tahiti or a campground or Disneyland, we feel joyous anticipation
- When we actually get to Tahiti or the campground or Disneyland, we have emotions of peace, excitement, and visual stimulation, not to mention the memories that don't fly out your wallet when you spend the cash.

Money also contributes to physical well-being and health: we can pay for health insurance; we can pay what insurance doesn't cover; we can afford wellness programs and gym memberships; we can pay for auto fuel and winter heat. (Or summer air conditioning if you're a desert rat like I am.) We can even have elective surgery to fix something detrimental or annoying on our bodies.

What non-money goals could you set, or help your reps set, if they don't already have them? Some examples are below. How can money enhance them?

- Providing your family with resources and experiences, whether it's camp or college or a cooking class in France
- Retiring early
- Becoming an expert guitar player (hint: lessons from a master, paying someone to clean your house or mow your lawn so you can practice more, etc.)
- Supporting a cause or helping others
- Getting promoted
- Having a bonded, happy and healthy family
- Expanding a homeless shelter

If our goals aren't about money, we can usually accomplished them more quickly, more easily and with better quality if we have a higher bank balance. This is true even if our goal is to give it all away.

The Sadder Side

A sadder side of the money goal is that many people don't feel they deserve more, or that they could ever attain more. They can't imagine themselves forging through the wall of their own value system or economic status, and their families and friends often reinforce their beliefs.

The election of Barack Obama as president of the United States sent yet another message that anything is possible in the USA. And it is. Obama's election, whether you supported him or not, is a profound example of how people can grow and become the person they want to be.

But let's get serious. A 45-year-old sales rep who is a single mom with three kids to feed may not relate to this icon of possibility. Her mind is probably absorbed with getting kids off to school or daycare, paying the bills, and showing up for work on time without vomit on her clothing.

You can help her escape from this cage of mediocrity. You can help all your sales reps change their lives by realizing they're capable of more than they think they are.

Multi-level marketing organizations (MLMs) are experts at this. Most of their meetings are filled with speakers who had walked through the doors with nothing other than a minimum-wage job, and who are now mulit-millionaires. They show pictures of the homes they came from, then flash on the screen the mansions they now live in. Then they basically say, "You, too, can do what I did, but only if you *want* it."

They raise possibilities for people who think they have none. They tell people they *do* have potential and that they *can* do it. And they add the magic word: *want.*

I realize that your sales reps probably earn more than minimum wage, and that in their current job, or even at your company, they may not become multi-millionaires. But we can learn a key message from MLM's that sales managers are wise to spread. That message is that you *can* succeed and earn more, give more or be more if you *want* it.

You have one more piece to add to this crucial message you send, establishing the foundation for all your work. It is embodied in the following words you can say to your sales reps:

"You *can* succeed and earn more if you *want* it,
And I'm going to help you."

PART II
Managing and Coaching: It's All Up to YOU

It often happens that I wake up at night

and begin to think about a serious problem

and decide I must tell the Pope about it.

Then I wake up completely

and remember that I am the Pope.

Pope John XXIII

CHAPTER 11
Push and Pull Strategies

When my daughter Janae was a teenager, I once came home to find her eating spaghetti. Then I noticed copious streams of spaghetti dripping from the kitchen ceiling. I wasn't at all amused, but I was definitely curious.

She told me, without cracking a single yes-I-know-this-was-stupid smile, that when spaghetti is done, it doesn't stick to the ceiling.

Before I could decide what my reaction was going to be, I realized that I felt like I was doing a similar thing at work—I was investing budget in training and waiting to see if it would stick. The only difference between Janae's actions and my own was that I hoped my spaghetti would stick, while she hoped hers would fall to the floor.

Throwing someone into a training class doesn't necessarily translate into enlightenment and change. Simple mandates don't work either. How do we get salespeople to do what is needed on the job?

Have you ever asked yourself that? Of course.

Wouldn't it be nice if you could just tell reps to change their behavior, and they'd do it? Picture yourself now, driving behavior by making pronouncements such as:

- "Mark, please increase your prospecting by 50%."

- "Sally, I'd like you to consistently recommend multiple products."
- "Joe, your servicing time is much too high. Starting tomorrow, decrease it by three hours per day, and spend that time prospecting."

As you know, those directions don't work. And yet, they're actions similar to what you probably want and need your reps to take. How do you get there? Shout it from the rafters every day? Install aromatherapy? Threaten torture?

The real issue in these three examples is behavioral change. Since all of us work on changing our behavior in some way, we know it can be difficult. For reps in the field, it's even more challenging because of the demands of their jobs, the market and competition, the number of products they need to know, and the habits they've developed.

That last item—habit—is the most difficult to overcome, but usually it's the only one you can change. Notice I said *you* can change. It's the reps' habits that are modified, but I assure you it won't happen if you don't initiate it.

We need to take ongoing action if we want change. Yes, I know, you don't have time. But investing in behavioral change pays big rewards later, both in revenue and time savings.

There are two kinds of strategies you can use to bring out (or drag out) the behavioral potential in your sales force. I call them the Pull Strategy and the Push Strategy.

The Pull Strategy is the enticer, the helper, the coach. We get into people's heads to help them understand where they can make more money, and how to get over those costly, automatic habits.

Many habits can seem benign but really are toxic—like yakking a few extra minutes at the coffee shop instead of calling on just one more prospect. (This teeny example would cost you 250 prospecting calls missed per year. If you have 10 reps, that's 2500 contacts or 250 sales at a 10% close ratio.)

With the Pull Strategy, salespeople must want to change, and they must already know how to do what you're asking. They must be motivated enough to follow your advice or decide on their own to change behavior.

The Push Strategy, on the other hand, is the accountability check. You push off their rose-colored glasses to reveal reality, and you push accountability for new behaviors that you require. If you don't measure and inspect, you can't reinforce and expect.

For best results, we need both strategies at play. But by thinking of them separately, you can balance your management and coaching to get the best results.

A manager who uses only the Pull strategy will train, reinforce, motivate, and coach, then wonder why it's not working.

If only the Push strategy is used, a manager can get so caught up in measuring, monitoring, requiring and forcing, that reps lose their internal drive, and your sales culture suffers. It can lead to short-term results with long-term disaster, such as high turnover.

Have you ever wondered *why* your sales training doesn't work well enough—why not enough spaghetti sticks?

It's simple. Sales training doesn't work because we shut it off at the end of the class. We don't use both Pull and Push. Salespeople can too easily sit through class, get great ideas and promise themselves phenomenal new results, then return to their territories or cubicles and crash back into the same old ruts and habits.

Salespeople must get out of their comfort zones and do something they're not good at, so they can practice and learn. How many of us want to do things we're not good at? If they were already good at these behaviors, you wouldn't have invested in the training in the first place! So holding them accountable for using new behaviors, through the Push strategy, is critical.

Let's face it—knowledge isn't enough. If we want a different skill set and more effort in the market, it's behavior that must change, and you're in charge of making it happen. Your job begins the moment training ends.

What Sales Reps Need from Managers

You may be the official person to evaluate and coach your sales reps, but they are constantly evaluating you, too. Maybe even more so.

While they may not verbalize it or think about it, they really want you to help them get better. People in general want to succeed. They want to perform well and feel pride in their accomplishments and in what they give to the world. And they want a supportive manager. But they also need and want someone to hold them accountable for bringing out their innate potential. And that's you.

What does that mean to them? Providing bagels or trips to Madagascar? Holding contests for recognition and tickets to the movies? Developing team spirit? These actions are good, but helping each rep develop more skills and talents is overwhelmingly more important.

We all want to keep getting better at what we do, but it especially includes sales reps. Besides the financial factor, it makes their jobs easier, more fulfilling and less stressful. That in turn leads to an enhanced personal life and a better basis for their future.

If we can sell, we'll always have a job, regardless of what happens in life. You literally have an opportunity to add to the lives of these individuals.

You can even eliminate your budget for loudspeakers, aromatherapy, whips, and a few trips to Madagascar because you'll already have what you need: A Pushing and Pulling You.

CHAPTER 12
Coaching vs. Managing vs. Both

I'm now mentally giving you a little poke—to get your full attention for this section. It can change your results and make your job easier. Here goes:

One of the most important keys to a sales manager's success is differentiating between coaching and managing, and knowing when and how to do each. Coaching and managing are two distinct roles you have, both of which are critical.

The following breakdown demonstrates this differentiation:

<u>**Managing:**</u>

Role: Evaluator, decision-maker

Goal: Get results, i.e. meet quota, improve close ratio, improve revenue per sale

Key Driver: Accountability, problem-solving

Examples of when to manage reps:

- When you've already coached, and they know how to do what is needed
- When you've already coached and they *should* know how to do what is needed
- When the behavior is not related to sales skills, i.e. arriving on time

- When they're disrupting the productivity or attitude of others

Coaching:

Role: Teacher, mentor

Goal: Get *behaviors* from sales reps that will get the results you want. What specific new behaviors and habits does the sales rep need to meet quota or improve close ratio?

Key Drivers: Changing habits, teaching

Examples of when to coach reps:

- When they don't know how to do something
- When they're developing or improving a sales skill
- When they're avoiding a behavior that drives revenue
- When they need to practice a skill (Hint: Stay with them while they practice, so the new skill can start to become a habit.)

Coaching is your teaching role, managing is your accountability role. Sometimes you perform them separately; sometimes you perform them back and forth within the same meeting with a sales rep.

In differentiating between coaching and managing, think of an analogy you can relate to, such as a personal trainer, a piano teacher, an athletic coach, a parent, an academic teacher, etc. Each has the same two roles of coaching and managing. One role is to teach and observe and help and practice (coaching); the other is to insure accountability that they *do* what you have trained (managing).

Generally speaking, you *coach* when your rep needs to learn or practice a skill. And you *manage* when the issue involves something they already know how to do—or they *should* know how. You've either spent enough time training, or it's a behavior they just need to *do*, such as arriving on time, using skills they've learned, turning in reports, following up, or using your systems.

Right now, think about one of your sales reps. Keeping the differences between coaching and managing in mind, would you say that this rep needs more coaching, or more managing? Or both?

If you selected to manage this salesperson, it doesn't automatically mean that the sales rep is in trouble, or in a warning phase. But it might. If you feel you've coached or nagged ad nauseam, it's time for this rep to go out and do what you know he/she is perfectly capable of doing. It's time for managing.

A savvy way to handle coaching vs. managing is to explain the concept to your sales reps. You can then explain what you're doing in each conversation. Example: "John, I'm changing to managing, and away from coaching, because you've shown me you know how to handle prospecting. Congratulations. Now we're going to shift to quantity of prospecting, where it's up to you to *do* what you know how to do. It still might feel uncomfortable at times, but trust in yourself because I know you can be effective."

Once you reach the managing phase, you save time. You're no longer teaching and helping as much. You're following up, reminding, checking, and giving feedback. In the behavioral sciences it's called reinforcement.

I've worked with many sales managers who explain this concept to their sales reps. It cuts through a lot of wasted discussions, wasted time, and insecure emotions on the part of your salespeople. And don't be surprised if they start thanking you—for being straight with them, for coaching them, and even for managing them.

The Soft Side vs. The Hard Side of Managing

How tough or soft should a manger be to insure success? Which is better?

Most of us are caring people but may not know how much to reveal at any given time, or in general. After all, we might think, employees could take advantage of our soft side. It's a common dilemma. A motto in the teaching profession is, "Don't smile until Thanksgiving."

Reps do need a manger who is caring. They need you to provide plenty of recognition, care about them as a person and encourage improvement.

But that doesn't mean you can turn into Pushover Patty or Wimpy Will. That would be akin to wearing a sign that says, "Ask me. I'll say YES."

Likewise, most reps need and want managers to hold them accountable for doing things that help them develop their skills and earn more. Sometimes that means being tough. If I'm your sales rep and you let me get away with doing less than expected this month, we both suffer consequences. It turns your future expectations into mere suggestions etched in runny soup.

For maximum success, there are times for softness and times for toughness. We need to be adept at using both at the same time. (This is not the same as Push and Pull strategies from Chapter 11.)

In my first sales management job, and without any leadership training, I needed to fire a salesperson. It was terrifying. I had no "firing" skills, no training and no experience. I thought I had to be mad at him before I could fire him. I couldn't be both tough and soft.

This doesn't mean you spontaneously switch personalities. If you're phony or inauthentic, it will show, and you'll wrap yourself in an extra layer of stress by not being yourself.

It's surprisingly easy to be both soft and tough at the same time. **Here's the key: Be soft on people, and tough on issues and accountability. Differentiate between people and behavior.**

Mental separation of people and accountability has spawned a motto of my own: We can do anything in business and life while still treating people with respect.

Examples of areas for toughness:
- Amount of prospecting
- Inhibiting work habits
- How they treat others or respect others
- Following your sales process
- Attendance or punctuality issues, including my pet peeves of arriving late for meetings and holding side conversations.

Some ways to use the soft touches are:
- Providing recognition and feedback
- Having compassion for personal difficulties

- Staying positive yourself
- Listening to truly understand
- Encouraging improvement

When the situation calls for toughness, never use it alone unless safety is at stake. Used alone, nothing can be heard above the *perceived* roar in your voice.

If safety is at stake, have back-up present. I once had to fire someone for abusive behaviors toward his employees, which was categorized under Violence in the Workplace. I was surprised to find out that our HR people insisted a security guard attend the final meeting between him and me. It seemed unnecessary, but there's no downside risk in taking safety measures.

Here's an abbreviated example of a soft/tough conversation you might have with an inbound sales rep:

"Chris, congratulations on your revenue. You've stayed productive; your customers like you; and I really appreciate your effort.

"My concern is your up-selling and cross-selling effort. I gave you additional help, and you said you'd keep practicing, but I've seen no change."

"You have a lot of expertise to offer your customers, and I know you can do it. But I do need you to change these habits. If you don't significantly improve within the next week, I'll be forced to…" (Provide the consequence.) "Do I have your commitment, Chris?"

Then put teeth in your deadline by setting a time for your next discussion.

Being tough and soft at the same time is effective in the most positive way possible. In fact, it's a lot like being a great teacher. But I do recommend smiling before Thanksgiving.

CHAPTER 13
Game Plans for Various Types of Performers

Are you a "fair" manager? Do you spend your time equally with all your reps? Do you allocate precious resources with equality in mind? We might automatically want to say, "Yes!" After all, Thomas Jefferson wrote in the Declaration of Independence that all people are created equal.[8]

But you're not running a country; you're running a sales organization whose mission is to increase profits and drive a strategy that helps your company thrive in the market. That means allocating resources for the best return. We can't always give everyone the same.

The most common misuse of resources is found in how managers use their own time. And your time is your most valuable resource.

Under-Achievers

Frequently, managers spend too much time with low performers—not those who are new to the job, but reps who are consistently at the bottom of rankings. These reps have enough knowledge and experience to perform better, but they don't.

---

8   Yes, I know he wrote "all men." I'm bringing President Jefferson into the 21st century.

Too often managers avoid taking action and continue developing and coaching. Why is that? What's the probability of changing results? Usually it's low. Reps may be mismatched to the job but can't admit it, even to themselves, and usually they feel miserable and stressed. Or they're unwilling to put in enough effort to get past coasting on mediocre results.

When managers spend an inordinate amount of time with under-achievers, whether out of caring, hopefulness or because of company policies, they must then reduce time with reps who have potential for generating even more sales. They lower their return on the investment of their time.

What is a manager to do? The answer lies in differentiating between coaching and managing. Coaching is teaching, and managing is evaluating and decision-making. If you've already spent sufficient time coaching someone, yet nothing has changed, it's time to *require* change. It's time for managing.

We must also make sure we're focusing totally on behavior, not on personality or personal characteristics. It's easy to get lax with this differentiation. We're not in charge of changing people.

If you think your rep Carol is too sloppy (and you're very neat, of course, so it drives you nuts), ask yourself why it matters. And it might, if she's wasting time looking for misplaced proposals, or has her own eccentric system that would affect whether someone could fill in for her in case of emergency.

So first, identify specific behaviors that are preventing success. Here are some examples spanning both inside and outside jobs:

- Not enough appointments
- Not enough calls handled
- Average length of call is too high
- Not enough cold-calling, or initiating
- Selling primarily their favorite, easier-to-sell products
- Lack of enough needs analysis, or order-taking only
- Low adherence to schedule
- Insufficient prospecting or outbound calls
- Not asking for the order
- Time spent complaining with others
- And okay, lack of organization

After identifying, respectfully communicate your requirements, along with the consequence of not improving. Frequently reps will ask for more product training, more coaching and more time from you. This may be a delay tactic based in fear, whether they realize it or not. If you've already worked with them fully and appropriately, the responsibility for change is now theirs.

So don't get sidetracked! You can say, "Lenny, you already have everything you need. Now it's time to practice and make a bigger effort. I'm confident you can do it, and now is the time."

After this conversation, following through with Lenny is essential, or you're sunk. Without follow-through and reinforcement, we lose all progress and we set a dangerous precedent. Review results and measurements to determine whether Lenny is improving adequately and then provide feedback, hopefully with encouraging news.

But if you've gone through this process with Lenny three consecutive times, in a timeframe that meets your company requirements, and without adequate behavioral change, some decisive action is needed. Lenny can either improve or it's time to send him off to other pastures.

Think of this as equal opportunity for all. It isn't fun, but it is fair. It's fair to everyone involved—your other sales reps, you, and the company whose revenue you are charged with multiplying. It's also fair to Lenny, who may become a happy, high performer in a different environment.

And because you would use the same method with any low performer, you are, in effect, treating all people equally. I bet even Thomas Jefferson would agree.

High Performers

The Gallup Organization[9] has done in-depth research about managers' impact on top sales performers and salespeople in general. Let's focus now on top producers.

---

9   Benson Smith & Tony Rutigliano, *Discover your Sales Strengths* (New York: Warner Business Books, 2003)

One of Gallup's findings is that sales managers have a tremendous effect on retaining top performers. These high performers apparently are confident enough of their skills that they won't stick around if they feel their manager is impeding their earnings. But with a good manager, they stay.

Managers also have a big impact on the *performance* of top producers.

Good managers help them flourish. With less effective managers, their results can decline. What's scary is that even with average managers, top performers sell less! This demonstrates, once again, the importance of your job.

How do top sales reps determine whether their manager is good? Is it whether they like them? Is it whether the manager springs for muffins, buys pizza or gives them the best cubicle?

Gallup found that sales managers are "good" when they help reps improve results. It's a nice touch if they like you, too, but that's not the deciding factor.

Right now you might be scratching your head thinking, "But my top reps are prima donnas. They want more from me, they have more customer problems and they complain about processes a whole lot more than my other reps."

If so, that's not unusual. High performers want more from you because they want the road slick, to enable selling at their capacity. They may have more customer problems because they have more orders! And they may complain more because every administrative bump can decrease their earnings.

Is it your job to give them only as much time as you give to others? No. A manager's job is to make that road smoother for them, even if you're giving them more than their share of time. (Often a problem you solve for them will benefit your other salespeople, too. They're just on the "bleeding edge" of discovering the glitches.)

After all, you're protecting a big revenue stream, and you're working at keeping those high producers on your payroll, not on the competitor's.

Besides wanting to hold onto top producers because of the revenue impact, there is another critical reason. According to Gallop, the customers of your highest producers are statistically much more loyal than other customers.

How do you know whether you're providing your top producers, and your team as a whole, what they need? How can you make sure you're influencing them in effective ways?

It's easy: Ask them. Whether you ask in a one-on-one meeting, in a group meeting or with a survey, ask them.

But don't ask, "Am I doing all right for you?"

Instead, ask, "What can I specifically do better or differently to help you sell more and enjoy your job?"

At first they might joke uncomfortably and answer, "Lower my quota."

If so, laugh and continue with "Seriously, I'm evaluating myself, and I really need your insights." You might be amazed at their perceptions.

High Performers who Don't (Fill in the Blank)

It's not uncommon for sales manager's to have conflicted feelings about high performers who, except for the soaring sales they bring in, want to dive under their desks when they see them approaching. Maybe these reps disrupt sales meetings, or they think they have immunity from following selected policies, or they expect everyone to care more about their orders than anyone else's.

More frequently, it is because their high performers aren't doing the amount of prospecting that you and your company require, precariously believing their current handful of customers will last forever.

We'll use an example of Mandy. When you coach or manage around this issue, Mandy responds by telling you to look at the latest sales reports, thank-you-very-much. Mandy has built up a few accounts that keep ordering and ordering, and Mandy's key priority is to bond with those customers and service the heck out of them. You're then stuck balancing your fanny on a two-edged sword. Do you keep holding Mandy to your prospecting requirements, or do you give in, happy to have Mandy's high performance?

Before taking a stand in either direction, ask yourself some questions such as:

- Is there more potential in Mandy's market? How much?
- If you gave Mandy more resources in support, would you be using her talents better?
- Do you need to give someone else the territory Mandy is ignoring (assuming she has an assigned territory)?
- How does your compensation plan affect Mandy, if at all? Would she feel fully rewarded for charging after more?
- What are the implications of each of your options? Is there company policy or precedent that you need to know about?
- How would Mandy herself handle the dilemma from your perspective?

This last question might be an eye-opening one for Mandy, and she might even give you valuable input or ideas as you develop a solution. Just be sure the solution you develop is one that you both stick to.

It's very important to wake Mandy up. She needs to get out of her cozy mindset and realize that she is living precariously. How? By hearing the call of reality. No sale lasts into perpetuity; we need to keep prospecting, whether it's within our one account assigned, or with many companies. Help Mandy realize all the risky scenarios that she is counting on *not* happening, such as:

- A merger that causes a change in vendor
- New management or the retirement of a loyal decision-maker
- Priority changes, either at your company or with the clients
- Entire product lines or divisions that are dropped because of new technology
- Global competition, or even local competition
- Bankruptcy for unseen reasons
- Sweeping compensation plan changes

I've known many salespeople who have lost over half of their revenues in one fell swoop. One entrepreneur I met had banked 80% of her sales with her biggest customer: The United States government. All of a sudden that sales stream evaporated, for whatever reason, and she was left standing in the dust in shock, realizing that she hadn't been an "entrepreneur" but rather a contract worker. If we want steady income, we need to diversify, and that means waking up to reality.

High performers who have slacked away from sales-driven behaviors still need you to hold them accountable for their own success. If you don't you're taking those risks right along with them.

Category 2 Performers

Have you ever said to yourself, "Whew! At least I don't have to worry about Bob, Jim and Meredith. They always meet their quotas."

You may not need to "worry," but Bob, Jim and Meredith may hold un-mined gold.

I call them Category 2 performers. They're not the highest achievers, but they produce consistently.

Would you rather have a 10% increase from your lowest performer, or a 10% increase from Bob, Jim or Meredith? Which 10% would be easiest to obtain? Which would give you the most revenue per hour spent of coaching?

Usually it's your Category 2 performers because it's easier for them to change.

But take it further. Which of your Category 2 performers will be more likely to jump into the ranks of the high performers? You can rank them by attitude, selling potential, market potential, etc. Then start with the one who ranks highest.

Don't scare the pants off them, though. If you've always given them free reign, then suddenly start coaching, they'll spend more time worrying about why you're coaching than they spend working on their behaviors. Set the stage. Tell them you believe they can be high performers and set a joint goal of getting them there.

Right now, which of your salespeople come to mind?

Selecting Behaviors and Priorities

"I need a sales manager!"

These are words I've heard many entrepreneurs repeat. They're not announcing a job opening, however. They're saying they need someone who will help hold them personally accountable.

Ironic, isn't it? Many salespeople complain about what their managers require of them, while those entrepreneurs who have escaped accountability find themselves in need of it. Many even resort to hiring independent coaches who basically function as a manager.

The point is that we all need accountability, whether we realize it or not. We all need someone to help bring out the best in us, and to keep us on track with our own goals.

As a sales manager, it's important for you to stay aware of your important mission and role in driving behaviors, and in how you help others find success. But where do you start? How do you allocate your time? You can't be everywhere at once, so it's important to make sure you're always working where you'll get the most revenue for your efforts.

Let's turn the concept into reality with a quick process focused on revenue-generating behaviors. We'll end up with five columns of information that will ultimately show you which people, and which behaviors, will bring the most revenue for you. (For an example, go to Step 6 in Part IV, titled Short-Cut Behavioral Focus.)

In Column 1 on a blank sheet of paper or spreadsheet, list each of your reps in the order of their sales results, with your highest producers at the top. In the second column, list each person's sales results. Use whatever results are meaningful, such as a six-month revenue average, or last month's sales.

Next comes the critical part. In Column 3, list one or more behaviors that you'd like each rep to change—behaviors that would make the biggest difference in their results. Here are some examples, spanning both inside and outside sales:

- Asking more questions
- Asking about previous results from competitive services
- Making more contacts
- Recommending more than "the usual"
- Staying more visible with key accounts
- Making more formal proposals
- Taking better control of contacts

Be sure you've listed behaviors that can be changed, not personal attributes about who they are. If I'm a person who doesn't show a lot of emotion, your chances of making me gregarious are zilch.

In Column 4, calculate how much additional revenue each sales rep could achieve by changing or improving the behaviors you've listed. Mix your gut feel with your market knowledge, and be realistic.

Now sit back and look strategically at your list. What will you find, as you scan completed numbers in Column 4?

Usually we find that the biggest increases can come from those sales reps who are near the top of your list, but who aren't currently your top performers—the Category 2 performers we discussed. The same percentage increase in their market is worth more in revenue than the same percentage increase from people who consistently achieve less. They're also more apt to make the changes you need. But you may also have some surprises that change your direction.

This doesn't mean you ignore some of your reps and dedicate all your time to a few, but it does help you focus and prioritize for the biggest gains. And if someone emerges very low for potential gain, why is that? If it's not because of totally phenomenal selling, dig deep for the root cause. You might find other reasons, such as a need for territory realignments or policy changes, that could bring more potential to your company overall.

The best part is that you can discuss your goal individually with each sales rep, show them what their potential payoff is, and give your commitment to help them increase their success level. They still may not dance into the office each morning singing praises about you, but they'll definitely know why they have a sales manager.

It's an Investment with an ROI

Whether you're hiring or firing, coaching or managing, you're making an investment decision. You want the biggest return for the time and energy you spend.

Simultaneously you're helping your sales reps make investment decisions in their own time and effort. Some will invest more in focused improvement than others do, independent of your efforts. It's a choice they make themselves, based on their internal drive and motivation.

The overriding objective is to balance your investment with theirs. You need a return on your investment of time, an ROI for each hour you spend coaching. Go for the gold with sales reps who are also willing to go for the gold. You may not be an Olympics coach, but you have the same types of decisions to make.

CHAPTER 14
How to Coach

I'll bet no athletic coach ever said to a player, "Hold the ball differently when shooting. Here, I'll show you. Now go practice. I'll be watching to see how many points you score in the game on Saturday!"

Would that be ridiculous, or what? But it's analogous to what a lot of sales managers do. We observe John; we give feedback and suggestions; we even tell him and teach him what to do differently; then we go our merry way until the next time we observe him.

By then, John may have totally forgotten what we even talked about in our so-called coaching session.

Managing is not the same thing as coaching, as we've discussed. Managing involves analyzing, helping and evaluating. Coaching is teaching and creating new behaviors—behaviors that will bring results. With coaching, we teach, and we *make sure* our reps practice and use the new behaviors habitually. I don't like to say it this way, but I will: We're *forcing* them to practice. Just like a sports coach would do.

Most managers spend all their time managing and administering and fighting fires. Few I've met have any time left for coaching, and most don't know how to do it. That's probably the underlying reason why they don't do it often enough.

Think about athletic coaches. They make sure the players practice the right techniques (behaviors), and they watch and help until their players can execute correctly time and time again. They stay for practice!

We can't insure people will get out of their comfort zones and develop new money-making habits unless, and until, we stay for practice. If you've ever had a personal trainer, you know that you'll run longer or lift more weights when your trainer is right by your side.

It takes some time investment, but it also saves future time and creates more revenue-driving habits.

My first habit-creating experience was after graduating from college. I found myself teaching Spanish at Central High School in Omaha, and was utterly green and naïve about Life. The high school was three times the size of my hometown. It was a rich mixture of diversity, spanning wealthy students with family traditions of attending Central High, to inner city students with struggling lives.

I loved it. Except for the shock of being assigned two classes of beginning students along with the higher-level classes. Why? Because I knew I'd spend those two hours doing nothing but staying for practice. Learning to speak any language requires practice, and I could visualize ending each day with my tongue dragging home after repeating things like, "Hola, Paco, ¿qué tal? ¿Cómo estás?" about 400 times. And I did. Over and over again. Repeating, correcting, and rewarding.

And then a wonderful thing happened: The students learned. Their mouths developed habits, and the words didn't seem foreign any more. Nearly all of them got an A in Spanish on their first report card. I know some of them, if not many, had never had an A before. My heart fills up just remembering their reaction. All they'd had to do was show up. And all I'd had to do was lead them into practice.

A Simple Running Track for Coaches

Staying for practice is part of a very simple sales coaching process you can use. Since coaching is teaching, our model is based on how people learn.

Figure 2

The Coach's Running Track To Stay for Practice

3
Ask & Give Feedback/ Reinforcement

Make at least one full lap within a short period of time.

1
Teach

2
STAY for Practice!

I'm calling this process a running track for sales managers, because you need to stay on it for at least one lap, and preferably more. The more laps you run in a short period of time, the better you'll change the costly behaviors of your reps.

There are only three hurdles on your running track: Teaching, Practice, and Feedback/Reinforcement. (See Figure 2.)

At the Teaching gate, you observe behaviors and identify one or two most important behaviors each rep can make, not make, or change, that will bring the most results. The most common ones involve prospecting quality or quantity, identifying needs or goals more effectively, and time management. You *communicate* this with the sales rep and set up a plan for change (or teach them how to make the changes needed).

Next, it's time to stay for practice. Your goal is to watch mistakes, effort, and improvement in progress. You might observe contacts, monitor calls, or help write a proposal. But you *stay there* with them, keeping your mind, body and brain *there*, while the rep practices this new behavior.

What you're really doing at this point is making sure they *do* practice. Without this action, there's an extremely high probability your sales rep will walk out of your office and plop back into old behaviors. And with practice, these behaviors or skills do what? They get easier, and the sales rep gets better at them.

Immediately after watching practice, withhold providing your wise feedback—until after you've asked the sales rep for his or her opinion. "I think it went OK," is not what you want. Ask for specific details. What did they think they did well? What would they like to have done differently? They're probably their own worst critics, anyway, and asking for their opinion helps them learn to be more observant of their own behavior.

Now it's your turn. Give feedback, reinforcement, and guidance. Fast reinforcement helps cement change. Look for what's positive and how to make it better, *staying totally focused on the specific behavior(s) that you're working on with your salesperson.* If you wander into other skills and behaviors, you've wasted precious time. After all, you're working on the highest priority of skills, right?

(The only exception to this is when you find a salesperson lapsing back into old habits or behaviors you've already worked on with her or him. In that case, you may not have spent enough time on the previous skill, and your priorities with this person might change. Or, your salesperson knows what to do and how to do it, so you consider moving into managing instead of coaching.)

Now, and only now, you have finished one lap on the Coach's Running Track. Can you run another lap right now? As I've said, the more laps you can take in a short period of time, the faster your results will emerge.

With inside sales and call centers, you can make many laps in an afternoon. With outside reps, you'll need more planning and scheduling.

How many of these laps do you think you can run in a week or a month? Could you set a goal for yourself, just like you would do at a gym or on a real track? It may take a little time at first, but once you start seeing the changes in your sales team, you'll know it's worth it. *Habits will change because practice makes them easier.* Your laps will also contribute to your own coaching fitness, too.

Relay Coaching Laps

Since your lap-running does take some time, let's come up with a less time-consuming method for some types of behaviors.

Many times you can improve behaviors and results outside of selling skills themselves. This might include areas such as time and territory management, daily task prioritization or changing other habits that decrease wasted time and effort.

We'll use the same model, but with these coaching laps you hand the baton off to your reps to run part of the lap. What a deal.

Let's say you have salespeople who are busy but who aren't productive enough. (That probably includes everyone.)

You decide that the new behavior you want is for them to prioritize their day—you want them to plan their day, number their priorities, and follow their plan. But you can't watch them all day long, and just telling them to do it isn't staying for practice. You also don't want to spend time following up every single day. Here's an example of what you can do:

- Have them to agree to the daily prioritization, to be done the prior day, before leaving the office.
- Have them email you their plan for the next day, in order of priority. And I mean *numbered* priorities.
- The next day, they do the same thing, except they include results from the current day, with items crossed off.
- You sit back (ha) and get involved only when you don't get that email.
- All you need a memory jogger on your own calendar, so you can hop into action when/if you don't get that email.

With Relay Coaching, you delegate the Staying for Practice part of the coaching lap, without giving reps more work. All you need to do is take action *immediately* when you don't get those emails, and then periodically provide feedback and reinforcement. Especially at first, give them plenty of praise and encouragement. Yes, yes, yes, this may be perceived as micromanaging. Remind them of the bigger goal—to develop a new habit that helps them achieve more—and that it's temporary.

We could also call this Exception Management, or Exception Coaching, because once your process is in place, you need to get involved only with the exceptions—the times they don't show you they still have that baton.

Reinforcement

How do we make sure that sales reps keep repeating those behaviors and skills we've taught them and practiced with them? Reinforcement is the key, of course. Reinforcement is defined as increasing the probability that a behavior will keep occurring. You can call it following up, or tracking, or any nifty name, but it boils down to behavioral reinforcement. Even when something becomes a habit, reinforcement is still important.

Let's put this in real-world but simple terms. You basically want the sales rep to be thinking, "I need to keep using this behavior because I know my sales manager will find out if I don't, and then I'll be in trouble." Or, "I want to keep using this behavior because I like it when my sales manager compliments me."

The first example above is called negative reinforcement: The employees are in trouble if they don't follow the procedure they've learned. This applies more in managing versus coaching, because there's an ultimate consequence that could be eminent. "Be accurate in pricing or you'll ultimately lose your job."

The second example, with compliments, is positive reinforcement. Positive reinforcement is preferable and works better in most cases. And it totally applies to coaching.

Easy so far, right? Now let's add some other terms: Fixed versus Variable, and Interval versus Ratio. I'll explain them with examples from an inside sales organization.

Situation: you've recently helped sales rep Andrew improve his prospecting skills. You've stayed for practice, and you know he has an adequate skill level. Now you need to reinforce these skills, and make sure he continues to improve them. And Andrew needs to know you're going to follow up. You plan to periodically but consistently listen to recorded calls and give Andrew feedback. That's reinforcement. How will you decide on your reinforcement schedule? Here are your options if you're **coaching**:

1. Fixed ratio: you'll listen and give reinforcement for every tenth outbound call.
2. Fixed interval: you'll listen to prospecting calls every Wednesday morning, and then give reinforcement.
3. Variable ratio: This week you'll listen and give reinforcement after variable numbers of calls, maybe the 5th, 10th, 11th, 27th, and 32nd.
4. Variable interval: Andrew never knows when you're going to listen and provide reinforcement. He might think, "Gee, I never know when my manager might be listening, so I'd better keep doing what she taught me." This is the best kind of schedule, usually.

But let's say you have an employee who is consistently late for work, and it's a behavior that affects results or service. You'll probably be using negative reinforcement, and it must be consistent day after day. If you used Fixed Interval, Wednesday reinforcement, for example, Stacie could feel like she got away with being late every day except Wednesday!

Treadmilling

In working with the Coach's Running Track, you first need to define behaviors, as we've discussed. Many are easily uncovered; some are trickier and more obscure.

Have you ever peered out over your sales organization and noticed very busy people who weren't meeting goals, moving in the direction you wanted or making progress toward increasing sales? If you have remote salespeople, you can't peer out, but you can still uncover the same phenomenon.

I group these behaviors into the Treadmill Syndrome: running frantically, but getting nowhere except in the same two feet of space, with no reward. Reps with Treadmill Syndrome work hard but, based on results, not hard enough. Or not smart enough.

If we can identify when people are on it, we can lower Treadmill Time and increase results for the same amount of work. Maybe even less work.

I've identified two primary types of Treadmilling.

The first is doing inappropriate service work, or Service Treadmilling. It's about making automatic, knee-jerk reactions on handling service functions without exploring options.

Scenario: Phil, a current customer, calls and asks for pricing on a particular product. "Hey, Ed, would you fax me your prices on Product X?" Phil asks. "We're doing some brainstorming over here and wanted an estimate."

If Ed were a Service Treadmiller, he would jump off the phone and start pricing out Product X. He might spend time figuring out several rates, listing feature options, contract options, and other ways that Product X could be purchased.

Then he would fax it to Phil—or drive it over to Phil—and pat himself on the back for being so responsive to his client. At the end of the day, Ed's manager might ask if Ed had done his prospecting that day, and Ed would respond, "Are you kidding? I was tied up with servicing!"

In this example, what Ed called "servicing" may even have been a disguised sales opportunity. Because he didn't ask Phil any questions, Ed couldn't offer a real recommendation. He may even have missed a bigger opportunity by not asking to participate in Phil's planning session or what Phil's goal was. And he probably missed out on increasing market share while wasting time figuring multiple pricing options.

Ed jumped on the Service Treadmill and just kept running.

The second type is Sales Treadmilling, or selling in a way that doesn't drive the sale; it merely keeps us in motion and dilutes the probability of those sales.

Here are some examples of Sales Treadmilling:

- Leaving an appointment without scheduling the next meeting, saying "I'll call you after we get a proposal developed." Setting a next firm appointment, for a specific purpose, helps qualify the interest level of the prospect as well as shorten the sales cycle by preventing a month's worth of playing tag.

- Sending out a proposal. No proposal should be "sent out" without going through it simultaneously with the prospect, even if it's generated by your inside sales group. (You may recall my unsuccessful attempt at this.) We're throwing proposals into the air and hoping prospects understand them with no encouragement or benefit reinforcement from the rep. Plus, reps don't get to clarify or answer objections. If sales reps are remote from their prospects, there's plenty of technology available to have a live connection that includes a presentation.

- Dropping off business cards, or gathering business cards and then doing little or nothing with them. Some reps optimistically call this "prospecting" and wonder why their return is so low.

- Losing oneself in Social Media without a strategy or plan.
- Ineffective networking that basically turns into socializing, often in the wrong market.
- Developing collateral or tools that are already provided by marketing, even though they may not be exactly what the sales rep would have designed.
- Doing more than required to make a sale—which can be like using a jackhammer to crush crackers.

The sad part of Treadmilling is that it's a habitual behavior, done with good intentions and often with conscientious efforts. Usually reps haven't looked down to notice they're stationary, instead of moving toward more sales.

I hope you'll immediately recognize the answer to this dilemma: Teach sales reps specifically how to handle these and similar situations. With some observation and coaching on your part, you can quickly decrease your reps' Treadmill Time. After all, no one wants to be stuck on a treadmill—it takes a lot of energy and goes nowhere.

A Productive Rep Knows What You're Thinking

There's another part of wasted sales rep time that you personally might be causing, and one you can cure very easily.

How much time do you think is wasted by sales reps trying to guess what their sales manager is thinking? It can be their most favorite water-cooler or telephone topic, spreading stress from one rep to another.

What do reps want to know about your thoughts? Most want to know how you think they're doing beyond—beyond what the sales reports show. Beneath those sales numbers lies an ocean of questions:

- Does my boss really think I'm doing well?
- How much trouble am I really in for not meeting my quota last month?
- Is my manager still focused on that last goof I made?

- What is my manager saying about me to his/her boss and peers?
- Would my boss rehire me?

Many wise people have said, "No one should be surprised at appraisal time." Research has shown that salespeople crave feedback and a sense of accomplishment in their work. Often these two even surpass the desire for financial gain.

Where does the most important feedback come from? Of course, it comes from you.

In my early and inexperienced years as a sales manager, I thought that my demeanor told people how I felt they were doing. If I was supportive and happy and enthusiastic, surely, I reasoned, they knew I was pleased with their work.

But I was living in fantasy land. They merely thought I was a happy person in general and had no clue how I evaluated their performance, or where specifically I thought they could improve. My feedback through suggestions didn't count, by the way. They were just that—suggestions.

We need to give frequent and concrete performance feedback to sales reps, and it needs to be packaged tightly around our priorities and strategies. This is especially important in times of economic pressures, when more is required to garner every single dollar in the market.

How often should we give feedback? My belief is that it should be done nearly every time we have a substantive meeting with reps.

You may now be thinking, "Good grief! A performance appraisal at every meeting? How on earth would I get anything else done?"

It can actually be very simple, and it can be tied to coaching and lap-running, where you'll make even more impact. Effective coaching, as you know, includes feedback and reinforcement. Here's a sample dialogue of this process with Casey, a sales rep:

> *Manager:* Casey, you've been making improvements in probing and including more products into your recommen-

dations, which of course is our priority. I'm really pleased with your work overall. So let's talk about this past week.

Casey: OK. I've been working on asking more questions, and considering various alternatives. It's getting easier to ask about their business.

Manager: Congratulations. You must feel good about that. What have you been finding?

Casey: Well, I made some multiple sales, and twice they ended up buying something entirely different than what they thought they needed.

Manager: That's a good sign. Your sales were up eight percent last week over what you usually do. Is that the reason?

Casey: Actually, without those extra sales, I wouldn't have had any increase at all.

Manager: Good, Casey. It does work, for both you and your customers. You had been struggling with your probing, but I think you've crossed a big hurdle. I'm pleased with both your effort and your attitude. This week, review your training notes and take it a step further. Then at our next meeting we'll talk about what you've learned.

Product Selling vs. Consultative Selling

In my experience, reps frequently say they they're confused about product selling vs. whatever your definition of consultative selling is. They might blame you or the company for mixed signals, and they need help and clarification.

So what is consultative selling? It's merely a way to sell products or services, right? By identifying specific needs and goals, we can better identify specific benefits and value. Even with pure "product selling," we're selling benefits. Is there really such a big difference?

Most companies want their sales reps to increase the scope or effectiveness of the questions they ask. How in-depth or lengthy should this analysis be? That depends on your strategies, your market, what you're selling, and the value of the sale. It may take seconds, minutes or weeks. Make that decision based on what best serves your prospect, your profitability and your success.

The secret to effectiveness lies in the first words that come out of the salesperson's mouth when they're setting the stage. Those first words determine the path of conversation.

The underlying issue is that many sales reps, regardless of what training they've had, don't know what to do, or don't feel comfortable doing it, or haven't practiced. So they do what they've always done, which is to start talking about the promotion or product itself. The minute they open their mouths, product information and specifications spew forth onto their prospect—sometimes with great technical specificity. This may be exactly what you want them to do, but more often it is not.

How do we change that? Here is a simple process that will lead to success.

First, as a group (or with sales reps individually), have them decide on five ways to open a sales call. You can even make this list yourself. Here's an example: "John, I thought of you for a new promotion we have, but let's save time by first discussing the priorities you have right now. I know your business has been changing fast. OK?"

This is the sneaky part, because once the reps start a sales call this way, they're forced to ask questions about need before they talk about the promotion or product.

Then, have each rep select two mini-scripts they like best, perhaps one for a new prospect and one for an existing customer. They can edit them to match their own style, but the message needs to drive toward the same result: qualifying the prospect by asking questions about needs and priorities.

Have them memorize these two openings *and* role-play them with you several times. They don't need to be memorized word-for-word, but well enough to flow naturally so they don't have to think about words they're using. After role-play, have them file, hide or throw away the scripts, or save merely a few key words, so they'll be natural and not canned.

What will happen when you announce the role-playing part of this step? Your reps will all try to talk you out of it. They'll say they don't need it, or that they're already doing it, or some other slippery excuse.

But role-play is crucial, because it's the very point in which you begin to change behavior. Don't let a single person off the hook, no matter how successful or seasoned that person may be.

Make these opening statements a standard and an expectation in your organization. Rent this behavior. You then enforce it through observation and feedback on every contact you observe. Remember that you are the one responsible for producing the change. The key is that once something becomes easier, we're more willing to do it. If we keep doing something, it becomes a habit. If it's a habit, we've successfully created a new behavior.

This course of action can end complaints about product selling vs. consultative selling, at least for the probing function. If it doesn't, haul your team back to role-playing and stay with them while they practice yet again.

If You're Less Experienced Than Your Sales Reps

But what can you do if you're still new, or you're less experienced than your reps? It's not uncommon for managers to have sales reps that are better salespeople than the managers themselves. Managers are promoted for their leadership potential, not merely for their selling savvy.

These top performers are people who may be most motivated to improve, so don't avoid helping them. How you coach, though, may be different. Certainly avoid making any statements that sound like:

- "You're doing great; you don't need me or my time."
- "I'm the boss now. You'll do it my way."

I've worked with many experienced, high performers who are elated with their new, inexperienced manager. Why? They're getting support, caring and respect. And they still want to improve!

If you're a less-experienced manager, how can you coach these reps? Here are three ways:

- Acknowledge their experience and expertise, and again, ask what you can specifically do. They'll tell you.
- Don't ignore them — spend time with them. You'll learn, you'll advance your experience through them, and you'll be giving them recognition.
- Offer them successful ideas you've observed through other reps. (And use with other reps what you learn from high performers.) Over time, you'll gain experience and credibility to provide valuable coaching.

You can also gain experience and expertise by learning from your peers. Ask as many questions as they'll let you. Just because you've become a sales manager doesn't mean you have to know everything. View your role as the catalyst for improving skills and habits. You can make an enormous difference, whether you're experienced or not.

CHAPTER 15
Change Your Thinking about What You Need to Know

If your boss comes to you and asks about a particular account, do you feel inadequate if you don't know the answer?

There is a disease that sometimes hits front-line managers that is called I-Have-To-Know-Everything. It hits every level of management, actually—the level of detail just changes.

With the front-line sales manager job, this disease is especially stressful and unproductive, burdening managers with unrealistic expectations of themselves. They can spend their days asking questions, holding meetings, requiring reports and spreadsheets, and pouring through information. It wastes their time and, more importantly, keeps reps cornered by too much administrivia and talking vs. doing.

At this point you might be asking, "But isn't it a manager's job to know what's going on?" No, it isn't. A manager's job is to drive the right behaviors that drive the most results. And yes, a manager needs quantitative and qualitative information about sales reps' actions in order to drive the right behaviors and results.

The critical question becomes what information, and how much of it, do we need? Where do you need specific account information vs. market information? Additionally, what is the most time-effective way to get it?

First, figure out what you need to know from a big perspective. For example, in addition to sales results and other benchmark criteria (such as trends in revenue per order), you probably want to know:

1. How well reps are prospecting and how much.
2. How well reps consistently follow your sales process.
3. How well reps sell all your products and increase market share.
4. How well reps implement and service customers, without wasting time and money.
5. Where you need to provide help, direction and coaching, or make managerial decisions.

Now re-look at number five above. It's the only reason you're doing the other four items!

Next, ask yourself to reevaluate how to find out easily what you need to know. Challenge yourself here, be creative and throw out all your assumptions.

For example, if a rep is surpassing quota and bringing in many new accounts each month, do you really need to know precisely how many cold calls he or she made each day and with whom? Maybe yes, maybe no. If you're unsure of the market potential in your reps' assigned territories, you'll want to know the prospecting levels of all reps, regardless of their results. A high *producer* may not really be a high *performer*.

One effective managerial strategy is commonly called the "helicopter approach." With this approach, you are the helicopter, flying around looking for problem areas or behaviors that need improvement. Then every once in a while, especially when you have an indication of something needing improvement—from observation or reports—you swoop down into detail, identify the cause, fix it and go back up in the air to keep surveying.

In real-life terms, assume you looked at a revenue report and find that Sally met quota, but barely. You also know she sells only her "favorite" products and doesn't sell enough targeted products. Rather than requiring everyone to report everything they're recommending on every proposal, you swoop down into Sally's terrain.

Your swooping could involve several fronts: riding with Sally, reviewing proposals with her and asking key questions after each needs analysis she does, side-by-side observation, reviewing recorded calls. Your goal is to uncover and then solve the problem. She could need help on anything from needs analysis, to recommending based on potential benefits vs. the prospect's stated budget. You may also need to run a few coaching laps with Sally.

And when your boss asks if anyone is working on a specific account, you can feel comfortable saying, "I don't know, but that's a good question. I'll find out." It's indubitably better than admitting, "I don't know. I'm not swooping there today."

CHAPTER 16
Three Success Drivers for Cloning Yourself

You've probably wished occasionally, or daily, that you could clone yourself to get your work done. How in the world is it possible for one person to handle your job and drive yet more revenue?

When you run out of time, what single category of work always gets tossed out? To use Stephen R. Covey's concept[10], it's the "important but not urgent work." This usually includes coaching time and other work critical to driving change and more prospecting.

A manager's level of productivity affects how reps work, too. If Sales Manager Char frantically bounces off the walls and accomplishes little, her sales reps may either model her or avoid counting on her. But if she provides a good example of time use, she can ask for and expect more from reps. Let's face it, there's no chance they'll prospect more without wise use of time.

But you can indeed create another you, or more of you, without actually resorting to cloning technology. Your time gains center on three different success drivers: (1) your goals and priorities, (2) focus, and (3) task timing.

---

10   Steven R. Covey, *The Seven Habits of Highly Effective People* (New York: Fireside, 1990), p. 151

Goals, Strategies and Tactics

We'll begin with goals and priorities, which set the tone for everything you do. Start there to immediately make a difference. Define your monthly, quarterly or annual goals. These should include not just revenue quotas, but what you personally want to accomplish, and what strategies you'll use. A strategy is a general plan of action or process that helps you meet your goals. We can have strategies around specific commission plans, or prospecting plans, or account planning, or selling processes. Any key direction for improvement can be a strategy.

Individual sales managers can have strategies around coaching, or productivity, or hiring, or market coverage, or recognition, as examples. The reason strategies are important is because they keep us on track and away from doing things that won't drive us toward our goals. In other words, they save precious time, which is the reason we'd like to clone ourselves in the first place.

What few strategies would make the biggest difference in your revenue results? What would make the biggest difference in meeting your personal goals? Probably all of them require an extended timeframe to complete. Determining your goals and strategies may require some analysis such as the following:

- Market analysis
- Behavior analysis
- Pipeline ratios (i.e. the number of prospects or proposals required to make a sale; revenue per sale, close ratio per person or industry or lead)
- Modification of procedures or expectations
- Identifying non-productive work you can potentially off-load from reps

You may already know deep inside you what your best strategies and goals are. Once you identify those key strategies, ask yourself what tactics and actions you need to take in order to bring your strategies to life.

Let's say you want to meet 110% of your quota this year. That's your goal. After doing your analysis, or based on your current knowledge, your strategies might include:

- Increasing by 50% the quality of probing your reps are doing, and
- Increasing revenue from cross-selling within existing accounts by 20%.

After developing your strategies, you need tactics. Tactics answer the question of how you'll implement your strategies. What will you *do?* Here are some examples of tactics for the first strategy shown above—improving the quality of probing:

- Review our sales training and sales process in a group meeting by March 1.
- By April 1, determine where we most need to improve, through observation, proposal reviews and team feedback.
- Set up specific change plan for three sales reps, get their commitment, and complete by May 15.

Notice that your goals and strategies are measurable. They *must* be measurable in some way, even if you are subjectively measuring. An example of subjective measuring is: Increase my personal rating of my team's proposal writing from a 5 to a 7 out of 10.

Tactics, on the other hand, are actions. They can be measurable or merely something you do, but give yourself a deadline. You can also separate your tactics into smaller action steps.

For example, assume you have a customer loyalty goal related to product delivery. One strategy might be to provide early notification to customers of potential delays in their orders, and you want to accomplish this strategy using as little of sales rep time as possible. A tactic might be to have support reps, or service reps, call customers when a critical or large order is in jeopardy of late fulfillment.

Every day, or every week, review those strategies and then ask yourself, "What can I do *now* to move myself closer to completing these strategies? What can I begin, or move closer to completion?" Make a list of these actions or select just one action for your *now* moment.

Daily actions should be part of a monthly plan. Take your end goal and determine what benchmark actions or goals you need to accomplish each month. The process is no different from planning a kick-off event, or a party, or a wedding—with small and frequent steps that get you to your destination. In our example of the customer loyalty goal, actions might include determining perimeters of an automated jeopardy report; requesting the report; and training service reps how to use the report, including when to escalate critical problems to you or your salespeople.

Part IV, Your Big MACK, has tools to help you develop your plan.

Above all, regardless of how flawed or perfect your plan is, keep it simple and visible. Put reminders on your calendar, and allocate specific times to work on it. If possible, have someone hold you accountable. If you decide to bury it in your briefcase, files or computer, you might as well save some space by tossing it in the trash. I know this from personal experience.

Focus Focus Focus

The second cloning method is through focus. Most of us are bouncing around from one thing to another, whether we cause it ourselves or whether it's thrust upon us by interruptions and too many things to do. One of the reasons for doing a strategic plan is to keep ourselves focused on what we're doing. But focus also applies in *how* we do something, and in what order.

We all have some sort of To Do list we put together each day, whether on paper, in a software application, or in our heads. But usually we leave off the most important action: *prioritizing each item the list!*

So here is the most critical action for your list: Number each item in order of priority. Always, and I mean always, do this. Urgent actions are first—urgent to your success—and the strategic ones follow shortly. If you use a software program for your daily list, most of them don't allow prioritizing. The last one in is the first one out. You'll be handsomely rewarded if you take the time to prioritize.

Meeting a deadline is urgent; coaching is not. But if coaching never gets on the list as a high priority, it doesn't get done. You already know this—you've undoubtedly watched coaching time fly out of your day many times. Adding to this pot of stew is the fact that we love to cross things off our list, and we migrate to the easy things first. Without prioritizing, you may be leaving the key to your success on your To Do list.

So force yourself to prioritize. Start with the first priority on your list and diligently, obediently, work downward. Don't allow yourself to skip around or sneak peeks at lower priorities on your list. Now look at Figure 3. It is a visual demonstration of how focusing can diminish all the extraneous annoyances that accompany your day. Things that are gnawing at our sanity can significantly fade away. Having fewer annoyances means less stress!

Hyrum Smith, values-based time guru, said that prioritization creates inner peace, which he defines as always knowing we're working on our highest priority.

But before you count on experiencing that inner peace, count on interruptions. We can't keep our minds glued to an activity in progress while the world appears to be crashing down around us.

Interruptions can be the bane of our existence unless we manage them to the extent possible. Consider these statistics from various studies you'll find readily on the internet:

- Time lost to email interruptions costs 26–28% of a person's work day
- Unnecessary interruptions can cost 28% of a knowledge worker's day
- The lost time with email interruptions is 64 seconds, while phone interruptions cost 15 minutes. This doesn't account for all those interruptions of people stopping by your office.
- Dr. W. Edwards Deming[11] said, "The average American worker has fifty interruptions a day, of which seventy percent have nothing to do with work." Dr. Deming's work, by the way (or BTW), was done before the advent of our pervasive emailing.

---

11   Dr. Deming, 1900-1993, was the father of the quality evolution.

If you feel you're working an extra day per week just with time lost from interruptions, it's because you probably are. Or you're losing a day's worth of productivity each week. Your sales reps probably are too.

What if you set up just an hour of uninterrupted time for everyone each day? Just one little chunk of time, when you are free from interruptions that aren't urgent. This time must also be free from chitchat about ballgames, babies, barbeques and everything else.

Can't many interruptions be delayed for a single hour? If reps use that hour working through priorities—like calling prospects for appointments—they'll gain about two or more hours worth of progress each day. I'm not exaggerating.

Then communicate, communicate, communicate. Tell your habitual interrupters that you and your reps will be unavailable during that time each day, and why. If they survive when you take a week of vacation, they can survive without you for one hour each day. Close your door during that time, if you have one. If not, set up a visual reminder, maybe even a sign. One sales rep in my training speculated smugly that a barrier of police crime tape might be appropriate.

Even with a focused hour set aside, you'll still get interrupted, right? After you've handled each interruption, immediately return to the priority you left. Don't let yourself feel deflated and start rummaging around your list. You'll waste tons of time and add to that feeling of overwhelm.

Can you guess who many reps say is their biggest interrupter? Yes, their sales manager. So be mindful of how often you interrupt your sales reps with something that could be held for later.

Stay vigilant about focusing on each priority during your entire day, both with your own "brain use" and with interruptions from others. Here are some examples:

- Don't needlessly do more than one thing at a time, or hop from one task to another. Stick to your prioritized list, which hopefully you are making daily.
- If reps repeatedly ask you questions they should know the answers to, don't quickly answer their question, but

address the bigger issue of how they can find the answer for themselves.

- If people ask you to make decisions they can make themselves, avoid bailing them out. They'll soon learn not to waste time asking.
- Delay interruptions: "John, let's talk about this at our next meeting."

Does this work perfectly? No. Can it make a difference? Yes.

You can help tremendously in keeping your team focused in other ways, too. One big way is: Don't feed the bear. Yes, you have multiple priorities you must pass on to reps, but show them how each one fits into major goals. Remind them of your major goals again and again, and make sure they know what you want, and how well you want it done.

During my corporate life, our sales organizations were once asked, yet again, to make some forecasts for a potential new product. Another interruptive Priority du Jour.

It took a lot of time and energy, so the opportunity cost was huge. Everyone made their forecasts with the precision we knew "they" wanted. We were all good soldiers. The time spent in getting the momentum back again was also costly.

A month later, I found out that "they" had rounded our forecasts to the nearest million. Nearest million! We probably had people obsessively forecasting to the nearest cent. And ironically, our forecast was so high that they hadn't believed us and cut it in half. When the product was then introduced, we couldn't fill the orders on time, and we frustrated and angered our customers.

Moral of the story: Sales management and marketing can significantly contribute to, or harm, a sales team's productivity. Again, don't feed the bear. If a task comes from higher in your company, ASK about expectations, priorities, and what amount of lost productivity the task is worth. Then make sure you communicate the level of effort you need for any given request. The big "they" in the sky might even change their minds about the value of their request.

One of the most useful sayings I've heard is, "People treat you the way you teach them to treat you." Teach people to help you focus, and teach yourself too.

Figure 3

Keep staring at the black dot.

**Soon the gray haze will
appear to shrink.**

**Focusing on our goals can
shrink obstacles and annoyances.**

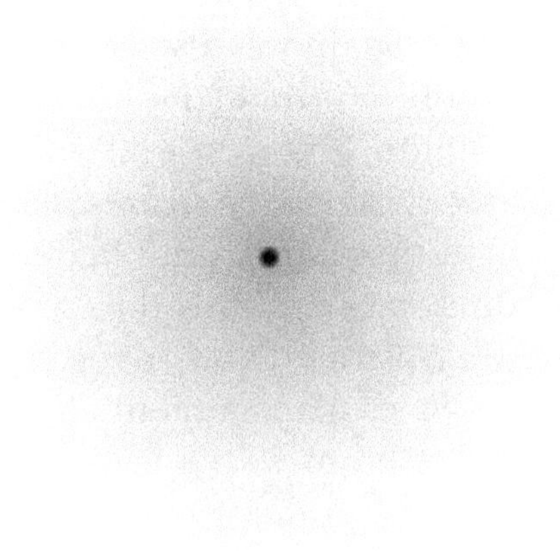

Task Timing

You've probably watched how an unpleasant item on your To Do list can repeatedly slide from one day to the next, even when it's high on your priority list.

After the third day, it starts smelling like spoiled meat. You keep smelling its constant aroma, but you always find something more important or more urgent to do, and you knock it off its prioritized pedestal.

We're heading into our third success driver: task timing. It's one more way to get closer to "cloning ourselves" for accomplishing the best possible results in our time available.

The spoiled meat phenomenon described above is affected by task timing. It occurs with two types of items:

- Items you don't want to do, or items that are unpleasant—such as addressing performance issues with a sales rep
- Non-crisis items. Coaching, of course, falls into this category.

What happens when we procrastinate? We feel nagging guilt at the back of our minds, sending messages such as, "You avoided it again, you idiot!" Or, "What's wrong with you?" Or, "Poor me! There's too much to do!"

These negative messages affect our overall attitude and our quality of work, whether we feel it consciously or not. We become frustrated, overwhelmed or disgusted.

The same thing happens with your sales reps. Some of the tasks they avoid are: giving customers bad news, discussing credit problems, and prospecting.

Prospecting is also their primary important-but-non-urgent item, and one that many salespeople want to avoid in the first place. This doubles its probability of ongoing procrastination.

The solution, for both you and your reps, is to use what I call "task timing." First, know when your energy is highest. To use a TV analogy, let's call it prime time and non-prime time. For most people, their prime time is first thing in the morning. Others say they peak around 10:00 a.m.

Second, use this prime time for doing items you've procrastinated. Make progress before the day's avalanche hits you, when you're at your peak.

Let's say you've put off discussing a difficult issue with a rep. Address it head-on, first thing tomorrow morning. You could set up the meeting right now and make it your #1 priority tomorrow. I'll wait while you schedule it.

(Here's non-interrupted 15-Second Intermission for Dialing and Scheduling, or Emailing/Texting.)

How does it feel to have that scheduled? Pretty good, I'll bet.

Now, let's say that tomorrow morning has arrived, and you've had your discussion. It was on your schedule and there was no reasonable way to weasel out of it. How do you feel? Proud of yourself? More energetic? More effective? Yes.

When we conquer those difficult or pesky issues right away—even if it's just a portion of one of them—a magnificent thing happens: Our attitude and energy levels surge for the entire day. We get more done, and the result is the same as if you had cloned yourself for those hours or minutes.

For your sales reps, prime time is best used for prospecting, whether by phone or in person. They'll get the same improved attitude and energy increase. When they begin the day with servicing or implementing, it will needlessly steal hours or wipe out an entire day.

The second key is to do less important things during non-prime time — typically at the end of the day. Push into non-prime time all your administrative work: phone calls, e-mail, paperwork, etc. If you have to schedule a meeting about process, set it for 4:00 p.m.

Reps are amazed at how much servicing they get done when they hold it for the last portion of the day. With a self-imposed deadline of getting home on time, servicing usually whizzes to completion.

You'll discover amazing productivity increases by using task timing. And that spoiled meat smell can be gone forever.

PART III
Critical Stuff to Spread Around

CHAPTER 17
Stop "Trying!"
Language Drives Success

Picture this scene: You meet your friend Bob on the street and chat for a few minutes. Before leaving you say, "Hey, Bob, we're having a little party Friday night. Can you be there?" Bob answers, "That sounds really fun. I'll definitely try to be there."

Will Bob show up? I can predict with relative certainty that Bob will not grace your event with his presence. He has given himself an excused absence by using the word "try," and simultaneously told you not to count on him.

The word "try" is a hazardous word in our vocabulary, and I'm on a rampage to eliminate it. It should be used only as a noun, after someone fails at an endeavor, such as when a Little League baseball player strikes out. Then we can say, "Nice try!"

In sales, the word "try" is used all too often by reps and sales managers alike, not to mention its insidious use by everyone on the planet. It gives our brains an escape route for not committing and a justification for not succeeding. Here are some examples:

- "My revenue goal looks really high, but I'll try to achieve it."
- "I'll try to call him this afternoon."
- "Sure, I'll try to do more probing."
- "Yes, I'll try to make 10 cold calls every morning."
- "I'll try to have my reps complete this by Friday."

At this point you may be thinking, “But sometimes we can’t make a guarantee. We don’t know whether other things will interfere. We can’t always expect a commitment.”

What’s important is not whether we can guarantee success, but whether we set ourselves up for success. Eliminating the word “try” keeps our mind and body focused on doing everything possible to achieve success. We are much more powerful when we change the examples above to these:

- “My revenue goal is really high, but I’m doing everything I can to achieve it.”
- “I’ll call him this afternoon. If he isn’t in, I’ll leave a message and call again on Thursday.”
- “Sure, I’ll do more probing. I know I need to ask more questions, especially about operational costs.”
- “Yes, I’ll make 10 cold calls every morning on at least four days out of the week.”
- “My reps will complete this by Friday.”

Once you start listening for the “try” poison, you’ll find that it’s a raging epidemic in our lives. What is it costing us, in both revenue and satisfaction? Could it cost us 5% or 10% of our revenue? Plus it feels so much better to say, “I’ll do it” instead of “I’ll try to do it.” As Jedi Master Yoda said in The Empire Strikes Back, “Do, or do not. There is no ‘try.’”

Monitor yourself and others for a week and count the times you hear “try,” then make corrections as you go, in both your own language and in your sales reps’ language. I guarantee you’ll find benefits. Putting a commitment stamp on our actions brings us to the table of life with action, energy, and more success.

Goodbye for now. It’s time for me to ~~try to~~ make my sales calls. I mean, it’s time for me to make my sales calls.

✲ ✲ ✲

Here are six replacement options for the word *try*, in the sentence, “I’ll try to meet my goal.” Which one doesn’t fit?

- “I’ll meet my goal.”

- "I'll do everything I can to meet my goal."
- "I'm committed to meeting my goal."
- "I'm fully committed to meeting my goal."
- "I'll do my utmost to meet my goal."
- "So just kill me if I don't meet my goal."

Here are six replacement options for the word *try*, in the wimpy sentence, "I didn't meet my quota, but I tried!" Which one doesn't fit?

- "I didn't meet my quota."
- "I didn't meet my quota, but I did everything I could think of."
- "I didn't meet my quota, but I'm still committed for the next one."
- "I didn't meet my quota. Would you help me evaluate what I might have done differently?"
- "I didn't meet my quota but I know I did my absolute best."
- "I didn't meet my quota. You obviously set it wrong, Dorko."

CHAPTER 18
Optimism Creates Results

Are you optimistic? Most people will answer, "Of course I am!" But we may not have as much optimism as we think. More importantly, do you know your level of optimism and its effect on your life?

Research by Dr. Martin E.P. Seligman has shown that optimistic people are not only happier, but they also have more money, better health and more friends; they live longer; they succeed more at work; they do better in school; they win more elections. Optimistic sports teams even win more championships. Many people and authors will tell you the same thing, but Seligman backs it up with years of research and a way to test your own optimism.

In his book *Learned Optimism*, which I highly recommend, Seligman says managers can drastically affect their team's level of optimism. If you've thought you have little influence over your team, think again!

Seligman defines optimism as how we handle undesirable events or misfortune. Economic climates are certainly undesirable situations, to say the least. But we can describe them, as well as other limiting factors, in one of two ways:

- With what Seligman calls "learned helplessness" — the belief that we can't do anything about it, so why try?
- With optimism

Seligman says optimism has three different explanatory styles, each one related to how we describe an adverse situation or event. He can also measure each style. We might be optimistic in one aspect but more pessimistic in another.

His dimensions of optimism, or pessimism, describe whether it is:

- Personal
- Permanent, or
- Pervasive

Personal optimism shows up in how you feel about yourself, which leads to your level of self-esteem. Do you blame yourself or others for misfortune, or do you blame the situation? Compare these statements:

- "I did a good job with that prospect, but she wasn't ready to buy."
- "That prospect didn't buy. I knew I'd foul it up."

With the permanence measurement, we're convinced that nothing will ever change, regardless of what we do, so we might as well sit back and let the sky fall. Consider the following two statements relating to this desirable event: You gave positive feedback on a rep's effort. Both examples demonstrate permanence, but one is optimistic and one is pessimistic:

- "My manager is always crabby and never tells me I've done well, so I'm sure she didn't really mean it."
- "I appreciate the feedback my manager gives when she sees the work I'm doing."

With pervasiveness, one negative event sends a universal shock wave throughout our minds, which then seeps into other thought patterns and affects our future actions. Let's say a rep has an unreasonable, abrasive customer. He can view it as either situational or pervasive:

- "This customer is unreasonable and treats me unfairly. I don't like dealing with him."
- "##!! That meeting was proof again that our customers think they can get away with everything and treat us like dogs. Why do I even bother?"

While the above examples are hopefully exaggerated, many subtle points exist between extremes that affect how we feel and therefore what we do. If we feel we have no control, how much action will we take?

The key is to be aware of what you say and what reactions take place within your team's psyche. Our words are also behaviors, since they are changeable. And you know, my dear sales manager, that you are renting behaviors. When you hear your sales reps falling into negative words, politely coach them to rephrase.

The economic climate and many other events are out of our control. The good news is that you and your sales team can react to anything with thoughts and actions that increase your chance of success for both the present and the future. You do have immense control.

CHAPTER 19
Authenticity: We Want YOU

Almost anyone who has children will tell us they're each born with their own unique personality and gifts. This divine light inside us, or whatever you want to call our individuality, stays with us for life.

But during childhood we learn to hide and deny many of our feelings as well as our personality—we hide who we really are. I remember many childhood attempts to mold me; some were culturally appropriate, and some shoved out the real me. I'm sure you can relate to these examples:

- "SMILE, Jeffrie!"
- "Wipe that smile off your face!"
- "Act your age!" (And usually we're doing just that.)
- "Don't do that—you might get hurt!"
- "Don't talk to strangers!"

As adults we learn to change our behavior depending on the situation and our role. We might have a work face, a customer face, a mom or dad face, a daughter or son face, a spouse or partner face, a friend face.

Obviously we can't be the exact same person with clients as we are with our buddies. Yet, while we're in all these roles, does our basic core shine through? Is it obvious who we really are?

All people crave, and I mean crave, one thing from us: our authenticity. Employees crave it; customers crave it. They want to know that they're interacting with the real you, not someone playing a role and going through the motions. It leads to more trust and more openness.

Sometimes we don't even know whether we're being authentic or not. We can become so accustomed to being who we think others think we should be, or driven by a need to appear to be something we're not, that we've lost our awareness and spontaneity. And in those moments, we've lost ourselves—the greatest asset we have.

We can also be inauthentic in our roles of life. If we're in a bad relationship or a job we hate, can we really bring out the best in ourselves in other areas of life? Doesn't it seep out and affect nearly everything? I'm not suggesting we automatically jump ship. I'm suggesting we take action to resolve the issue, either externally or within ourselves.

Sometimes others see in us what we don't see in ourselves. Dr. Martin Luther King, Jr. didn't see the leadership potential he had. His friends saw it, though, and they practically dragged him into releasing his innate abilities.

What do your friends and colleagues say about you? What do they see in you that you might not see? When someone compliments you on a good trait or potential gift within you, listen and take heed.

The clue to knowing whether we're being authentic lies in our feelings—in whether we feel relaxed, free and fearless, action-oriented, knowing that who we are is all we need.

Bring yourself, your best self, to the table of your life. Then help others, especially your sales reps, do the same. The world is waiting for more of the real *you*.

CHAPTER 20
Conclusion: Your Super Hero Role

As a sales manager, you have a secret role as a Super Hero. You may be responsible for the revenue of your sales team, but secretly you dash behind a wall and don your Super Hero Behavior Perspective cape. You know your real mission is to mold and maintain behaviors of your team, and that's exactly what you're doing.

As a Super Hero, clad in your tights and cape, you fly into planned action:

- With your x-ray vision, you **identify** behaviors that need changing, or new behaviors you want to rent.
- With your hyper-focus, you **prioritize** and charge after behaviors that will make the biggest difference in revenue growth.
- You **communicate** your decisions and actions with your salespeople
- You then shift into high gear to **turn costly habits into new beneficial habits** that create revenue.
- You distinguish between **coaching** and **managing**, and you know when each is your best tactical maneuver.
- And you **stay for practice**, completing your mission by making sure these new behaviors become habits, and that sales reps are held accountable for maintaining them.

You then remove your Behavior Perspective cape and head off into the sunset, satisfied that you have fulfilled your mission. You feel an immense sense of accomplishment, because you know that today's behavior drives tomorrow's results, and that you—*you*—are accountable creating today's behaviors.

Well, okay, maybe I took that description a little too far. Then again, maybe I didn't. Many times I've witnessed the gratitude of people who now have, or who have had in the past, a top-notch sales manager. By continuing to improve your skills in this significant role, you're sending out shock waves of progress that affect many more people than you'd think—from yourself, to all employees whose salaries are paid through revenues, to the families of your salespeople.

Awesome.

> *"I must admit that I personally measure success*
> *in terms of the contributions an individual makes*
> *to her or his fellow human beings."*
>
> Margaret Mead

PART IV
Your Big MACK:

Managing

Action and Change

Kit

Rich people think in decades;

Poor people think about Tuesday all day Tuesday.

Gail Sheehy
Author of *Passages* and
Pathfinders

An Overview of your Big MACK

You can merely read this book, pick up an idea or two, then stash it on a shelf, or you can use it as a process for growth and rewards. It's up to you.

If you choose the path to bigger rewards, this section is your roadmap. It holds your Big MACK. Your MACK is your **Managing Action and Planning Kit**, which will guide you through the process of making change and driving new revenue-generating behaviors. It's big in terms of results, but little in terms of simplicity.

There is a logical flow in this process. However, you can use all of it, or just the parts that have particular importance to you in how you drive behavioral change.

With your MACK, you'll be more able to better manage yourself as well as your reps, bringing to life the concepts that will benefit you the most and create the biggest rewards in the shortest amount of time.

I'm sure that many of the answers for increased progress already reside within you. The MACK merely coaxes them out of your brain, in a way that provides clear focus vs. overwhelming frustration.

In each case I've included forms or examples of plans, so you can understand them more easily. Remember that there is one critical element that will insure your MACK works for you: knowing whether you've succeeded. And that element isn't measured by revenue.

Why? Because there are too many other factors affecting revenue, such as economic conditions, service delivery, new competitors, pricing changes and promotions, etc. So revenue results alone can make your team look better than they're really doing, or they can be doing a phenomenal job but appear to be spending their afternoons in the movie theatre. We *must* know how much and how well reps are prospecting and selling, and where they need to improve. It all relates to behaviors.

Another reason we can't look at revenue alone is because we lose critical time. By the time revenue reports arrive, it's too late to make a difference.

So ask yourself with every one of your actions and plans: **How will I know whether my sales reps and I are behaving with an appropriate amount of quantity and quality?**

As you begin this journey, it's best if you can spend some time alone without interruption. You'll need a quiet, calm brain to mine your gold.

STEP 1
Your Personal Goals

Your personal goals are the foundation for your planning. At this point, what do you want out of life? What do you want to achieve or accomplish in the next three to five years? What part of those goals can you complete in the next twelve months?

It may take some significant thinking to write these out, but if you don't determine what they are, whatever you accomplish will be less. We *want* before we *get.* It's the law of the jungle, and also the law of our brains.

Determine what kind of goals you're setting. A three-to-five year plan is often the best place to start. With a longer-term, bigger goal, you'll be more effective in looking backwards from your goal, to determine how to advance better right now.

These goals can revolve around financial gain for specific personal or family purposes, or they can be just to meet quota so you keep your job (not too invigorating but perfectly okay), to get promoted, to learn and grow, to help others, or to earn more money solely to give it away. What's important is that your goals are what *you* want.

Be sure you list items in a specific and measurable way.

The next page has a format you can use, but you can make up your own. Add pictures, drawings or color—your brain loves them.

Goal-Setting

Circle your Timeframe:
3–5 years
1-year
6-mo

Today's Date _____

My Top 3 Goals
How I'll measure progress and success for each

What hurdles I might need to overcome

What strengths I bring

Who else my goals will help

People or resources I'll involve to support me and hold me accountable

Specifically, how I'll set up my accountability

How I'll feel when I achieve these goals

STEP 2
Favorite Highlights

You'll now review any notes you made while reading *Straight to Great*, ideas you had, or highlights you marked, and especially any pages you started chewing while growling. This is your brain dump. These items might be:

- Beneficial things you used to do but have stopped doing
- "Aha!" moments
- Things you've known you needed or wanted to do
- Different perspectives you gained
- Areas you know can be improved

Examples might include:

- The concept of renting behavior
- Coaching vs. managing
- Daily task prioritization
- Multi-tasking vs. overlapping
- Staying for practice
- Relay coaching

Make a list of your favorites, and keep it handy while you proceed in developing your plan. This list serves as further ways you can implement more change with greater probability, and take action on special points you've learned. They'll also serve as mind joggers.

You can also write them on the next page.

Favorite, or Key, Highlights

Behaviors You Want

Now list the specific sales rep behaviors that will bring the most revenue success. First list the obvious ones, then dig deeper into more specifics. List them in terms of:
- Your sales process,
- Quantity and quality,
- Personal habits.

Then for each of the behaviors you've identified, rate each of your sales reps. This rating will serve as a reference point for you.

A. Sales-producing behaviors relating to **quality:**

B. Sales-producing behaviors relating to **quantity:**

C. Behaviors needed for **effectiveness** (time management, territory management, servicing time or quality, market coverage, teamwork, etc.)

STEP 3
Determining Your Strategies

We have discussed goals, strategies, and tactics, and you determined your goals in Step 1. If you made any notes at the time, use them here.

You're going to lay out your blueprint in this step, using the concept of a pyramid. (See Figure 4.)

Now that you have your thoughts and ideas in the forefront, along with all you know about yourself, your reps and your markets, it's time to use your gut instincts: What are the top three key actions that would make the most positive impact in your success? Where is the 1-2% that would create the biggest difference for you in meeting your goals? List them in terms of behaviors, action, *doing*.

What you want are big-ticket items that will make a difference and lead you toward your goals. They must be things that you personally have authority to accomplish. Let's say your goal is to achieve 110% of your quota, in order to get a bonus of $X, so you can (fill in the blank). A big-ticket strategy might be: Get low-producing territories at quota. Or: Improve average revenue per sale by 10%.

The question to keep asking yourself is: What will help you reach your goals? Select the big chunks, and keep it simple.

Write your strategies here, with only one to three for each goal you identified in Step 1. Don't work to "fill in all the blanks." The fewer strategies you have, the more focused you'll be. Just cross out what you don't need.

Figure 4

Strategy Pyramid

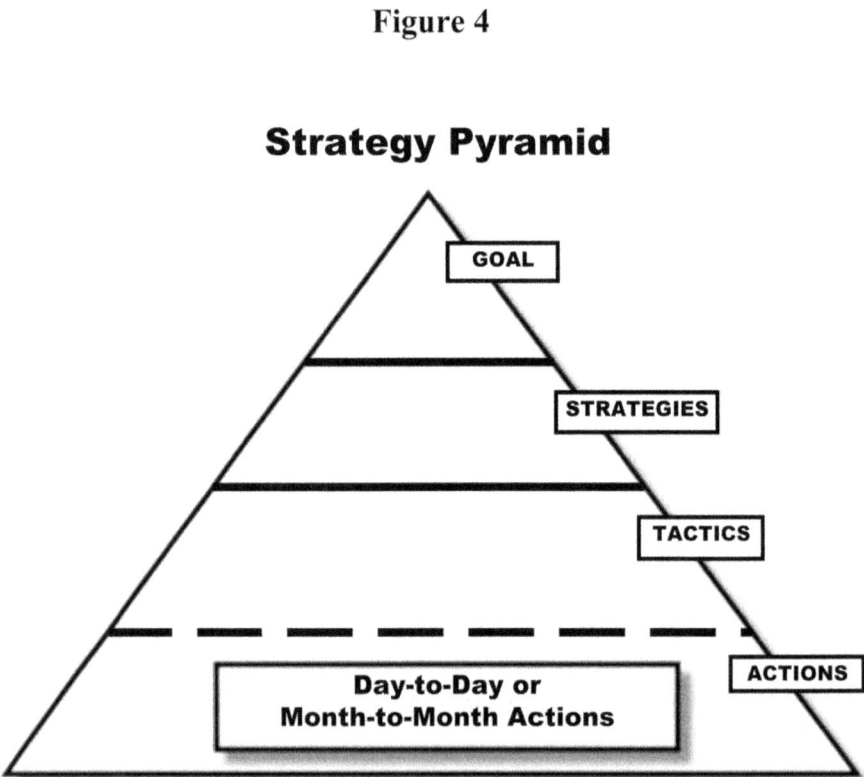

Goal 1:

Strategy 1:

Strategy 2:

Strategy 3:

Goal 2:

Strategy 1:

Strategy 2:

Strategy 3:

Goal 3:

Strategy 1:

Strategy 2:

Strategy 3:

STEP 4
Tactics and Actions

Tactics can be very easy, but make sure what you're doing fits in with your overall goals. Ideally, everything you do leads toward your goals. (See Figure 5.) Think about what it will take, in terms of *your own behavior*, to succeed with your strategy. Each tactic will then require some actions on your part to pull it off successfully. What are those actions?

Here's an example of a goal, a strategy, two tactics, and some actions.

>**GOAL**: Meet 105% of my quota
>
>>**STRATEGY**: Have each territory achieve no lower than 100% of quota, with three above 110% based on top reps' performance
>>
>>>**TACTIC 1:** Increase my group's prospecting quantity by 15%, in preparation for new habits needed in realigned territories
>>>
>>>>ACTION 1: Communicate with reps on renting behavior
>>>>ACTION 2: Review training and role-play
>>>>ACTION 3: Measure and monitor prospecting quantity
>>>
>>>**TACTIC 2:** Realign territories to better match market potential
>>>
>>>>ACTION 1: Do analysis of territories

ACTION 2: Redesign and get approval from boss

ACTION 3: Get reps on board with changes

ACTION 4: Figure out transition plan for current customers

ACTION 5: Measure and monitor improvement

The most important part of this step is to avoid getting down into the muck. You could spend a whole month making a deliciously beautiful and comprehensive spreadsheet that would win you Spreadsheet Designer of the Year Award. You don't want that award!

Figure 5

Example of Goal with Strategy, Tactic and Actions

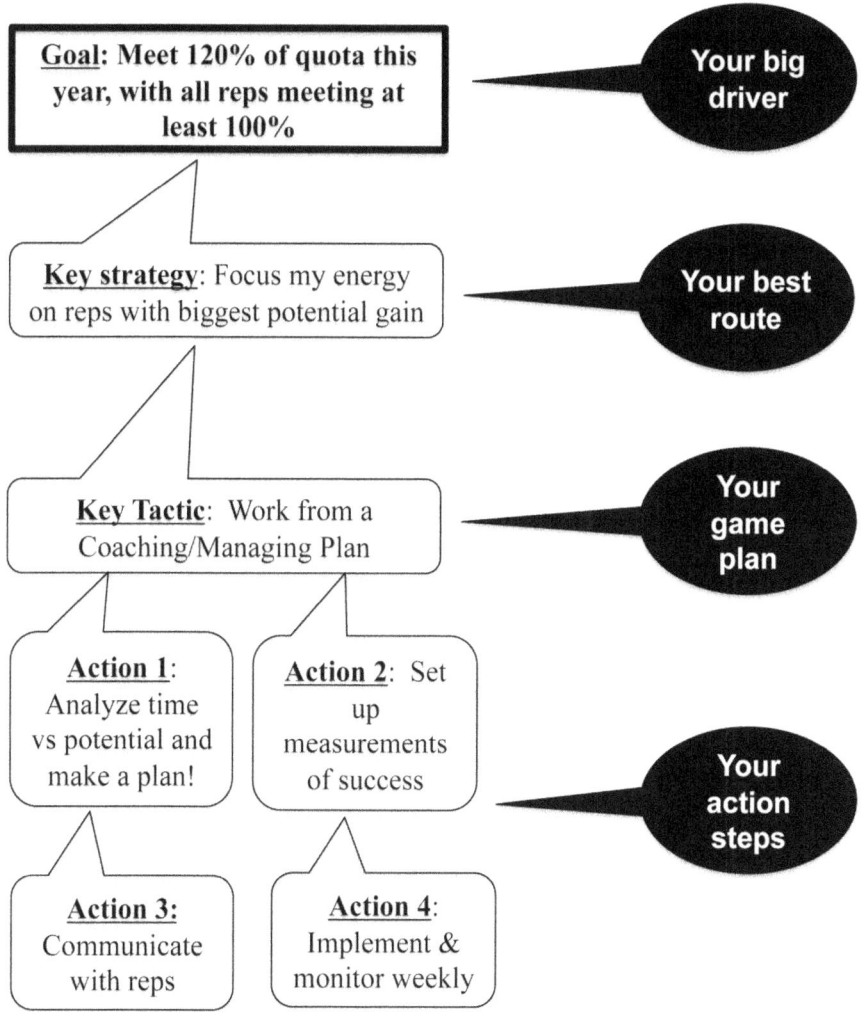

STEP 5
Coaching and Managing

Now we jump to another aspect: Identifying where to direct your efforts—which salespeople are your top focus right now. We do this to increase the Return on Investment of your time. Both this step and Step 6 relate to the return on your time investment. Step 5 gives you a more global perspective; Step 6 is a short-cut for immediate action. You can use either one, or both.

Whenever I work with manager groups to design their plans, they nearly always find they're spending too much time in areas that bring the lowest results, because that's where their "problem" lies. We can easily miss the potential gained from time spent with higher achievers who have a greater likelihood of making change and gaining bigger increases in overall revenue.

It's similar to having your sales reps spend their time with squeaky-wheeled low-potential prospects. It isn't done consciously, of course, but we can get caught up in our day-to-day work at the expense of the bigger picture.

This process helps you decide strategically where and how to spend your time. Then, when issues arise, you'll be more likely to make decisions grounded from your best approach.

But first, let's review the difference between coaching and managing:

- Coaching is teaching. The goal is to improve skills, and change behaviors and habits.

- Managing is evaluating and making decisions and directing. Our goal is to hold sales reps accountable for the behaviors we are renting.

Normally we'll do both coaching and managing with each sales rep, but there are times it's more appropriate to stick with one or the other. Here are some rough guidelines on when to do more of one:

- Under-achievers: Assuming they've been adequately trained and already coached sufficiently, strict managing is appropriate. They usually need to get out and just do what they know how to do, or do more of it.
- Above-average but not top performers: These are the Category 2 reps who are usually neglected, and they're the ones who can bring the most revenue per hour of your time. Coaching works well, especially if they want to achieve more.
- Top performers with experience: Either coach them or stay out of their way. But you both gain by spending time with them. You can learn from them, which will help you become a better coach for others. They also need reinforcement and recognition for their high results. They, too, can fall into habits that don't serve them.

In the following sample analysis (Figure 6), the manager has ranked each sales rep based on several criteria, such as sales results, market potential, attitude, etc. If you have five reps, force yourself to rank them from one to five, with either one or five being high. Average the scores for each rep.[12]

Then rank how much time you spend with each one. I know this isn't scientific, but your gut will probably give you the same answer that a month's worth of time tracking would.

There are many extenuating circumstances with this method, such as the account base, experience, problem accounts, etc. But you'll be able to factor those in as you determine how to improve the return on your time investment.

After you've completed the analysis, determine any changes you want to make, and take action. Share your intentions with

---

12   Ranking, not Rating, is used for this purpose. You might have five people rated as a Number 5 (highest score), if they're all performing extremely well. This analysis forces you to rank them from highest to lowest.

each of your reps, or involve them in the analysis of their individual potential. The more they know about what you're doing and why, the better they'll respond, even if the news isn't what they want to hear.

A Note on Rating vs. Ranking

Rating and ranking are two analytical tools you can use for many purposes, but it's important to differentiate between the two.

With *rating*, everyone is scored using the same measurement. If all your sales reps meet 110% of their quota, and you're rating them on a scale of 1 to 5, they would all receive the same rating. So let's assume we gave each of them a 1, or the highest rating.

In your analysis for prioritizing, however, we force a *ranking*. That means you would force yourself to rank the sales representatives from 1st place to 5th place. If they all still met 110% of their quota, and you were measuring on percent of quota attained, you'd start adding decimal points in order to compare the salespeople.

Let's assume these five salespeople had the following ranking and achievements:

1. Steve: 110.4% of quota
2. Mary: 110.25% of quota
3. Ahmed: 110.2% of quota
4. Lindsay: 110.05% of quota
5. James: 110.00% of quota

How will James feel if you announce that he came in 5th in quota attainment? Would he feel more recognized if you announced that he achieved 110% of quota? Likewise, would you recognize Steve if he achieved 1st place, with only 80% of quota? We need to be careful with ratings and rankings.

In general, use rankings when you need to force yourself to make a decision, such as who wins the latest contest, or which person gives you the estimated best return on your coaching investment. Otherwise, stick to ratings, where everyone can win.

Figure 6

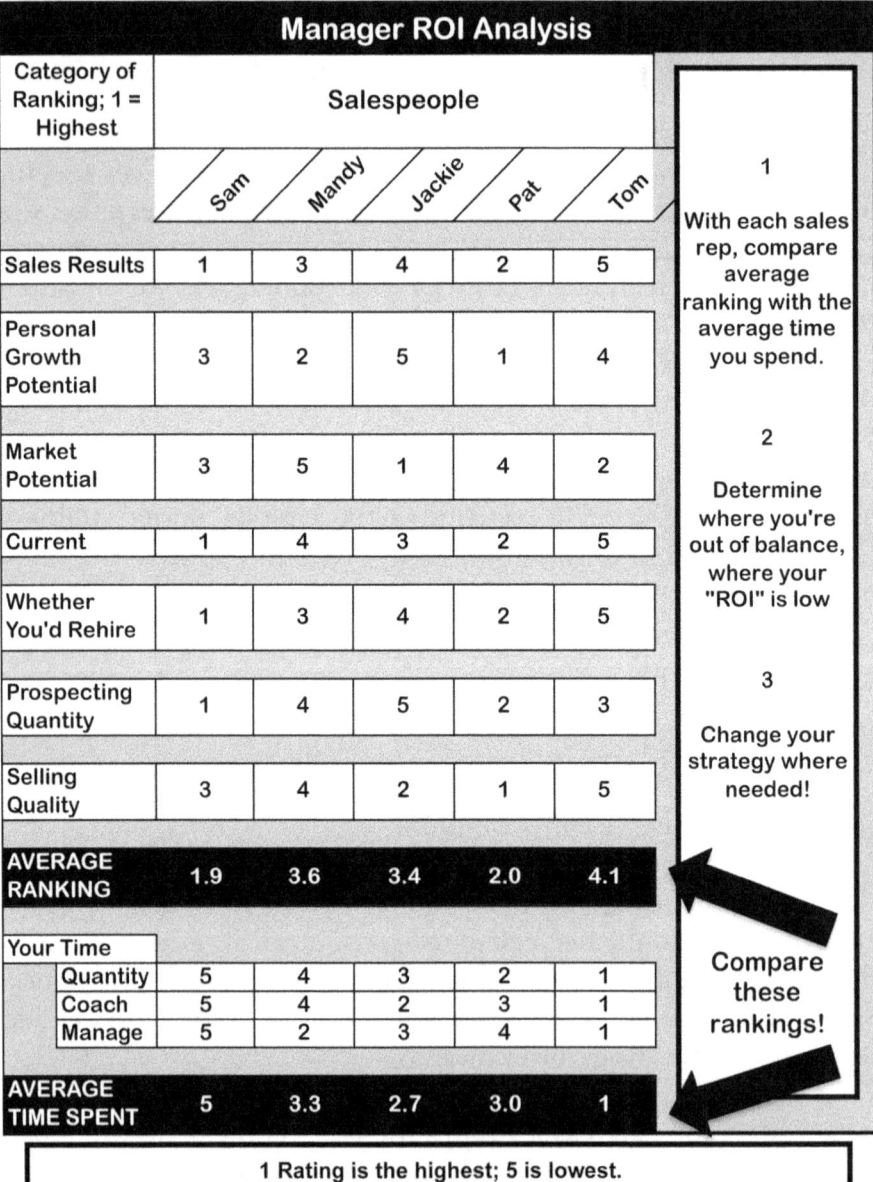

Category of Ranking; 1 = Highest	Salespeople						1
	Sam	Mandy	Jackie	Pat	Tom		With each sales rep, compare average ranking with the average time you spend.
Sales Results	1	3	4	2	5		
Personal Growth Potential	3	2	5	1	4		
Market Potential	3	5	1	4	2		2 Determine where you're out of balance, where your "ROI" is low
Current	1	4	3	2	5		
Whether You'd Rehire	1	3	4	2	5		
Prospecting Quantity	1	4	5	2	3		3 Change your strategy where needed!
Selling Quality	3	4	2	1	5		
AVERAGE RANKING	1.9	3.6	3.4	2.0	4.1		
Your Time							Compare these rankings!
Quantity	5	4	3	2	1		
Coach	5	4	2	3	1		
Manage	5	2	3	4	1		
AVERAGE TIME SPENT	5	3.3	2.7	3.0	1		

1 Rating is the highest; 5 is lowest.

STEP 6
Short-Cut Behavioral Focus

In Chapter 13, Selecting Priorities, we laid out a process for determining your coaching and managing priorities. You'll want to refer back to it. And as I stated previously, you could use both Steps 5 and 6, or select one of them. Step 5 develops a bigger picture for you—one that may give you bigger insights. Step 6 is faster and can be used to establish your monthly priorities. It also forces you to determine specifically those behaviors that will generate more sales.

The short time you invest in these steps will shower you with a plethora of benefits:

- You'll lower that feeling of overwhelm because you'll have a strategic perspective of where your time is best spent;
- Even on an unconscious level, you'll work more with sales reps who have a faster and more likely probability to bring more revenue;
- You'll be more effective by knowing when to coach, when to manage, and when to do both;
- You'll notice that you feel more in control;
- You'll have a better understanding of behaviors.

Short-Cut ROI Plan   Figure 7

Rep	Amount Over Quota	New Behaviors Desired	Potential Gain	Priority/Plan
Sidney	$30000	Discovering potential for lower-revenue products	$5000	Recognition only
Lee	$5000	Prioritize daily / Handle all servicing in the p.m., not the a.m.	$12000	Priority 2
Raj	$1000	Asking more questions / Taking better control of contacts	$15000	Priority 1: coaching
A.J.	-10000	Recommending more than "the usual" / Making more contacts	$10000	Priority 1: coaching
Campbell	-18000	Making more / Making more formal proposals / Recommending more than "the usual" / Asking more questions	$10000	Priority 1: managing only

Without this exercise, would you have guessed that Raj and Lee would be your top coaching priorities?

STEP 7
Your Action Plan

What can you do *right now,* to bring significant progress alive?

You're ready to put your thought process into a pinpointed action plan for a specific period of time, such as a month. Don't worry, you won't be plugging in every single item you've discovered so far. The point of this exercise is to make it reasonable. Your final plan should meet these criteria:

- Focused
- Simple
- Prioritized
- Realistic
- Bringing highest return on your time investment
- Driving you closer to your long-term goals

In Figure 8, I've laid out a sample format for one month. Figure 9 uses part of that format, with some example entries. I included these examples to demonstrate how to *measure and monitor.* When I work with individual sales managers, I nearly always find that the measuring column does not include a way to really measure the action. Be ruthless in quantifying your success. If you don't, you could be spinning your wheels, using a lot of your energy merely to cross something off a list. Your goal is to *make real change* in behaviors that lead to revenue.

You could design this for one quarter, but you'll change behavior faster if it's on a monthly basis. Each subsequent month would then merely be updated, not totally revamped. But be sure to refer to your overall goals, strategies, tactics and coaching priorities each time you update. It might be time to delete one action and move to another. In other words, stay on track with your bigger mission.

What kind of improved relationship and communication would you have with your boss if you share this each month? You might be amazed, and you might get tremendous support and ideas. You'll undoubtedly be viewed as a strategic, committed, action-driven sales manager who wisely and diligently drives today's behaviors for tomorrow's results. Why? Because you'll be one.

Figure 8

Sample Monthly Action Plan

Goal & Action	How I'll Measure and Monitor	Monthly Action Plan				
		Week 1	Week 2	Week 3	Week 4	Results
Personal Habits						
Targeted Reps						
Strategic Action						

Figure 9

Examples of Actions with Specific Measurements

Goal & Action	How I'll Measure and Monitor
Personal Habits	
Make Daily Prioritization a Habit	Do at least 4 times per week; Mark a star on calendar if done.
Call one customer per day to ask how we can increase value	Calls entered in calendar; Goal of at least 15 this month
Sales Reps Priorities	
Joan: More cold calls, Coach then Manage	Reports: meet monthly expectation
Jay: Better probing with C-level prospects, Coach	Help Jay prepare for contacts and role play; go on two contacts and let him handle! Measure subjective percent of improvement.
Gary: Increase rev/order with more cross-selling, Coach - staying for practice!	Reports and observation. Goal is 20% increase in two months
Strategic	
Identify prospecting potential in territories, for potential changes	Compare market coverage with amount of prospecting reps are doing
Identify Sales Call Reluctance® issues in group, including my own, and determine action	Complete the SPQ*GOLD Assessment and identify opportunities for improvement; develop actions for next month.

STEP 8
Daily Prioritization

Would you rather put out a fire with teacups of water or a fire extinguisher? For me, prioritizing has the same effect as the extinguisher—strong shots of action in the right direction. Many people have learned how to prioritize, from one time management course or another, but rarely do I find anyone doing it.

I'll freely admit it took me a long time to habitually prioritize my own To Do list, but I've finally reached the point where it's an almost seven-day per week habit. It's crazy that it took that long (and I'm talking about years), since it's such a freeing process. My cluttered brain gets more cleaned out before I begin working, and it stays much more focused during the day. I solemnly swear my productivity increases substantially through prioritizing every single task.

I now have the signs of a real habit: If I go in my office in the morning and just begin working or checking email, I start getting a little craving feeling, like something isn't right. It gnaws at me. Then I realize I haven't prioritized yet, so I stop and do it. The craving goes away, and I pat myself on the back.

I'll also admit that the only way I achieved this habit (and it's definitely an achievement) was by hiring someone to hold me accountable for doing it. Sad, but true. Maybe this isn't so sad. As I've said, we all need a coach; we all need a sales manager.

It's unfortunate that we need to prioritize so intricately, but an interruption epidemic is sweeping the planet. We have instant messaging, hand-held devices shooting emails to us, blogs, spam, ezines, texts, and changing technologies. Not to mention the rampant overload of information and increasing job responsibilities. Staying focused for even 30 minutes can require the discipline of a Marine.

We also have numerous other interruptions. We lose three minutes every time we change tasks or have an interruption. Most sales managers have around 20 interruptions per day. That's one full hour lost per day, or 12½ % of an eight-hour day. If time equals money, could we be losing the same percentage of revenue?

Prioritization of daily tasks is a phenomenally powerful tool for sending our brains into super-gear, and I've included my favorite format in Figure 10. Its basis is a visual mind map, which aids our brains in remembering and in seeing the big picture. I hope you'll use it (or some other method) daily as well as have your sales reps use it.

Here's how to set it up:

- Take a blank sheet of paper. I often use letter-sized cardstock, because it's easy to use and sends my brain a signal of importance. Start drawing in the landscape position. The center circle would have today's date.
- Identify four basic categories, which you can select. I have the top two as the most critical. In this example, I've used the categories of People (salespeople and customers), Strategic, Administrative and Low-Energy Time. The reason we separate them is to make sure we're not filling our day with too much from one category at the expense of others.
- List today's tasks in the appropriate categories.
- Then, ask yourself, "If I only get one of these things completed, which one is the most important?" Place the number 1 by that item. Then ask yourself, "If I only get two of these items completed, which is the next most important?" Place the number 2 by that item. Continue this process until all items are prioritized.

- Start your day working on number 1, of course, and proceed through the list. Now here's the power of this tool: When you get interrupted with something important, you can handle the interruption and then go back to where you were working. Don't let yourself skip around the list, looking for the easiest things to cross off. That's a luxury we can't afford.
- I often use a colored marker pen as I cross off my items completed. Our brains respond to color, and it gives you more gratification in completing your priorities.

Another way to stay focused on priorities is to use your daily schedule. In the first space that isn't filled with a meeting, add in your first priority. If you think it will take an hour, use an hour's worth of space. In the second space without a meeting, put in your second priority. Obviously, don't cross off your first priority until you've completed it, and don't move to the second priority until you've finished your first one.

Many CRM systems[13] keep your "to do" or "to call" items separate from your schedule (in addition to not allowing you to prioritize). For me this doesn't work, because it leaves us, once again, jumping from one list to another, spending time deciding what our next task will be. If you have this dilemma, you can list your important tasks as appointments.

These processes look simple, and they are. They're also very powerful and can make a colossal difference in how fast you reach your goals, and in how centered and focused you are on reaching your goals. The key behind them is also simple: the shortest distance between two points is a straight line.

13 Customer Relationship Management systems

Conclusion

You're now on your way toward doing two of the most fulfilling parts of life: giving and receiving—giving benefit to the lives of others, and receiving fulfillment along with rewards. You'll be creating your own special path of peace, joy, and abundance.

Bon Voyage! I wish you a tremendous journey.

"The best sales tool in the world is a great sales manager."[14]

---

14   Bruce Mihok, Vice President of Digital Marketing, Global Marketing, Inc., SAP

Figure 10

A Daily Prioritization Tool

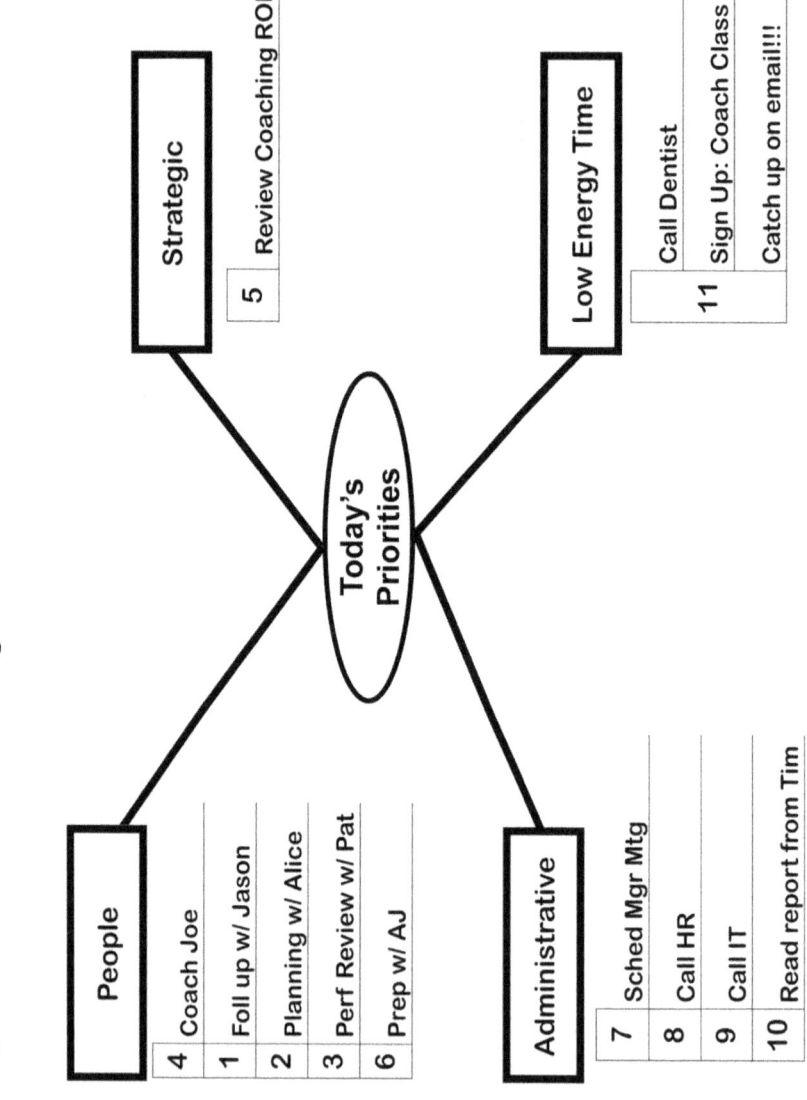

Resources Available from
Jeffrie Story
story@jeffrie.com
Unleash Your Sales DNA®, LLC

- SPQ*GOLD® assessment, which measures Sales Call Reluctance® behaviors, used in hiring, for development of current sales representative and to help sales managers improve their coaching and managing
- Fear-Free Prospecting and Self-Promotion Workshop®, the only training program in the world specifically engineered to help overcome career-limiting emotions due to Sales Call Reluctance® and developed by BSRP, Inc.
- COACHCAMP, developed by Jeffrie Story for front-line sales managers, which includes follow-up coaching
- Speeches
- Consulting
- Coaching
- Facilitation

www.ingramcontent.com/pod-product-compliance
Lightning Source LLC
Chambersburg PA
CBHW051525170526
45165CB00002B/611